The Preacher in the Emperor's Court

To Oliver
All the best
and love from
Dapping
x

The Preacher in the Emperor's Court

John Chrysostom

Dayspring MacLeod

CF4·K

10 9 8 7 6 5 4 3 2 1

Copyright © 2019 Dayspring MacLeod

Paperback ISBN: 978-1-5271-0308-5

epub ISBN: 978-1-5271-0375-7

mobi ISBN: 978-1-5271-0376-4

Published by

Christian Focus Publications, Geanies House, Fearn, Tain,
Ross-shire, IV20 1TW, Scotland, U.K.

www.christianfocus.com

email: info@christianfocus.com

Printed and bound by Nørhaven, Denmark

Cover design by Daniel van Straaten

Maps by Jeff Anderson

Contents

For Neil, who first took me to Constantinople.
Without him this book would never have
been written.

A Night Out on the Town

The evening's entertainment was about to begin. Full of excitement, John made his way to the biggest theatre in Antioch. Along the road his many friends and fellow students couldn't wait to greet him.

'John! Great speech you gave today in the marketplace,' one pal cheered.

'The great Libanius said you were going to succeed him as the best mind in the city,' said another, clapping him on the back.

John was glowing with his latest success. Everyone wanted to know the most talented lawyer-in-training in a city known for its great minds. Other young men gathered around him, laughing, each trying to make the cleverest joke. It was even more exciting than watching the actresses and acrobats at the theatre – because their future careers depended on showing off their wits in this way. And they also depended on knowing the best mind around, which was now John's. They didn't just like him, they had to be his friends. One day he might be their boss.

Only one young man didn't seem interested in either the theatre or the banter. John saw Basil across the market square, dressed not in gorgeous blue or pink linens, but in coarse brown cloth. He waved, and one of the other young men called out, 'Basil! Come and join us!' But Basil just nodded at them, friendly but uninterested, and went his own way.

The theatre was as brilliant as always, with its hilarious actors falling over themselves and its beautiful singers bringing tears to the audience's eyes – and its even more beautiful actresses flirting with the young men in the audience – but John couldn't stop thinking about Basil. They'd once been best friends. He was almost as talented as John himself, but there was something about him that was complete and content. He didn't need to rely on frivolous entertainment to distract him from his inner loneliness. Something told him that even if Basil's career didn't turn out as brilliantly as John's, he wouldn't be miserable about it. There was something noble about Basil. Watching the gorgeous actresses dancing in their enticing way, John felt ashamed to be there.

The shame wore off as he walked home with his friends, laughing about the night's performance. They'd all drunk several cups of *tsipouro*[1], and by the time John walked into his house, he wasn't walking so much as stumbling.

---

1. *Tsipouro* was a strong alcoholic drink popular in the Byzantine Empire, tasting of aniseed or liquorice.

His mother, Anthusa, emerged from her bedroom as John clattered through the door. Anthusa was still pretty, not yet forty despite having been a widow for twenty years – John's entire life. But tonight she looked older, pale and exhausted.

'Oh, hi, Mama,' John said, peering at her. 'You look terrible. Wearing yourself out working for the church.'

'Wearing myself out waiting up for you,' she said severely. 'Where have you been? You smell like drink.'

'Just at the theatre. Celebrating.' His face split into a grin. 'Libanius said I was the greatest of all his students! I can see our future. Me in the law courts, you running a household full of servants in our new house …'

'Libanius,' Anthusa repeated, wrinkling her brow. 'He may be the best professor in this city, but don't forget he also taught Julian[2] – and encouraged him to drive Christ out of the empire in favour of the old, false gods. Is that the man you want to base our future on?'

'Just because Libanius has taught me how to use my mind doesn't mean he's taught me what to think. And no one in the city can do more for my career than him.'

'Oh, son,' his mother replied, turning back to her room, 'will you ever learn what's really important?'

John shrugged and went to bed himself. He fell asleep imagining the wonderful things that were going

---

2. The last emperor, Julian the Apostate, had believed in the pagan Roman gods and had fought to bring them back in place of Christianity as the empire's official religion. He had studied with Libanius, who was also a pagan. His reign was brief and the new emperor, Theodosius, had returned Christianity to its full place of honour.

to come out of his mouth, the magnificent things that the people of the city were going to say about him. The future was his.

The next morning, John was just waking up after a long lie when his mother appeared in his room. 'John, are you up? A friend is here to see you.'

John sat up, blinking, as Basil came in the room.

'Morning,' he said. 'Mind if I sit?'

'Go ahead,' John yawned. 'Thanks, Mama.'

'I'll leave you two alone. Anyone for some bread and pomegranate juice?'

'No thanks, ma'am.' Basil pulled up a wooden stool as John's mother left the small bedroom. 'Enjoy the theatre?'

John shrugged. 'Same as usual.'

Basil nodded. 'I went once or twice. It's all right as long as you're watching, but you come away feeling empty.'

'Yes, that's true,' John smiled, fluffing his hair with his hand. 'But what else are we boys to do with our evenings?'

'There's always a choice, John.'

'Oh, I suppose I could stay home and talk to Mama. But it does mean something to be seen around town. People go to the theatre just to hear my witty remarks during the performances, you know.'

'Are you an actor?' Basil asked wryly, and John blushed. 'And it wouldn't do any harm to talk to your mother once in a while. She's one of the godliest women in the city. Even your great Libanius said she was impressive, and he's a pagan. Everyone admires her – that's a lady you can learn from.'

John laughed. 'You can't make a career out of being a Christian, however good you are at it.'

Basil wasn't laughing. 'The Church could use your talents.'

'What, are you thinking of becoming a preacher? Of all things, Basil! You could be a great lawyer too.'

'Who said anything about a career?' Basil asked. 'I'm not even worthy to think of the ministry. I'm just a student of Christ.'

'You're not doing a very good job of convincing me. I'm going to be the best lawyer in the city, and you're telling me to give up all I could become.'

'No. I'm telling you to become something greater. Something that will last after death. What do you believe in, John?'

John shrugged. 'I believe in my mother's God, of course. What do you think I am, a pagan?'

Basil tilted his head. 'You don't live like a man who believes in the God of humility and purity. You love the theatre and the games and horse races at the hippodrome. You love the law courts and arguing and nice clothes and good food.' He leaned in closer to John. 'And you are empty and unhappy.'

'And you think poverty is the answer to cure me?' John asked with an uneasy smile.

'I think you're like the rich young ruler who asked Jesus what he should do to be saved. He was imprisoned by his riches, full of fear of losing them. Remember what Jesus told him?'

'Sell all you have and give the money to the poor, and come, follow me.'

Basil looked directly into John's eyes. 'Sell all you have. Give the money to the poor. Come follow him.'

'Basil, I can be a follower of Christ without going to extremes.'

'Can you? Christ said that to follow him was to take up the cross. That sounds extreme to me. For that matter, he went to extremes for us. Do you really know, and believe in your heart, that Jesus died as a sacrifice so that God can forgive all your sins instead of punishing you for them, and that he rose again so that you can live a new life through him?'

John shifted uncomfortably. 'Yes, I know all that, but there are other things too. I can be a Christian lawyer. Not all Christians are called to the life of a minister or monk.'

'No.' Basil nodded. 'But I believe you are.'

A New Life

After Basil left, John had tried hard to forget all he'd said, his challenge that one could not be truly a Christian without giving up everything for Christ. That couldn't be right, could it? John knew plenty of people in the church who did other things as well. They couldn't all be the priest, after all. Some were soldiers, or builders, or servants, or tax collectors – they went to services on Sundays instead of pagan holidays, and gave their money to the Church instead of the temple. Wasn't that all it meant to be a Christian?

Yet John found himself staring with glum wistfulness at the baptised believers going forward for Communion on Sundays, and envying the sweet satisfaction on his mother's face as she listened to the Psalms, and resenting the times Libanius asked him to attend an important debate on a Sunday. And then at one morning service, the priest read out the words of Paul:

I have been crucified with Christ. It is no longer I who live, but Christ who lives in me. And the Life I now live in the flesh I live by faith in the Son of God, who loved me and gave himself for me.[1]

It was like being shot with a burning arrow. This was what Basil had meant: because Jesus had died for John's sins, died in his place, John now had to be dead to sin. His life had to be only in Jesus, or he wasn't really a Christian at all. He suddenly knew without a doubt that there would be no peace for him unless he gave Christ his all: his hopes, his future, his talents, his life.

* * *

Bit by bit, things changed for John. He lost his interest in the theatre and was soon disgusted at the thought of the silliness and wickedness that thrived there. It was not just a waste of time, he thought now, but dangerous – remembering how the 'actresses' tempted their young customers, and all the wine consumed, and how the name of Christ was taken so lightly. Even the law courts seemed meaningless and dull to him now. They were deciding affairs that belonged only to this world, and John was increasingly living in Christ's world.

He and Basil once again studied under the same teacher, no longer the pagan Libanius, who still worshiped the old Roman gods, but a devout old man who delved deeply into the truths of the Bible. Actually, studying the Bible was not so different from studying law. Debating the finer points of God's nature, or different interpretations of the same Bible verse, felt pretty similar to arguing about the interpretation

---

1. Galatians 2:20.

of the law. All the important people of the empire argued about theology[2] just as passionately as politics – and would even split into political parties based on things like whether they believed Jesus was God. So the discussions in the little seminary still felt exciting, and John still got a thrill out of making a witty remark that left the rest of the class speechless; it still raised a cheeky grin to his face. It was good to know that he could still enjoy using his mind and his clever tongue, but now do it for God!

But Basil did not seem so impressed. 'John, you need to be careful how you use that famous wit of yours,' he said sombrely as the two friends walked home one day. 'You argue so well that no one knows how to answer you even when you're wrong. You can make a bad interpretation sound good just because you put it in an elegant way. That's a dangerous power.'

'It's the talent God gave me,' John protested. 'It's a good thing to win an argument for him.'

'Theology isn't like law,' Basil replied. 'It's not about winning arguments or scoring points. It's about learning humbly how to follow God and lead others to him. And when you humiliate your fellow students like that, you drive them further from the real truths of Scripture. Your job now is to learn how to lovingly persuade people of Jesus' love, not to show off. The way you talk, people hear your voice – but they don't hear Christ's.'

---

2. The study of God.

John wanted to answer back with a barrage of arguments about how Christ had made his voice, and so he must be speaking through John – but that would only prove Basil's point. 'Humility,' he muttered. 'Right. But then how do I know when it's right to speak up at all?'

Basil smiled. 'Don't be offended, dear friend, and don't go to the other extreme. You'll know it's right to speak because you'll have words that point others to Christ, not to you. You need to stay quiet just long enough to listen to him. Then he can really use you.'

It stung to hear Basil's criticism, but the longer John thought about it, the more he knew his friend was right – he'd been proud, and he started to take the time to listen. To his surprise, he learned that his other classmates had good insights too, sometimes even better than his own. More than that, he came to see the ways in which they were like Christ: one of them especially generous, one of them encouraging, one of them passionately devoted to prayer. He started longing to see these things in his own life, rather than just the ability to make a clever argument.

As the two friends devoted all their time to studying the Lord's things, they heard some exciting news. The bishop of the city, famous for his holiness, was coming back to town. 'This would be the perfect time,' Basil said, 'to be baptised.'

John recoiled in horror. 'Baptised! You want us to be condemned forever?'[3]

'How can you say such a thing? Baptism is there to bring us closer to Christ.'

'The Bible says that baptism is for taking away our sins. Paul is clear that once we have come to faith we can no longer sin, and if we do, it's like we're crucifying Christ all over again.[4] But we are young, Basil! How can we possibly be strong enough to go through life without sin? We may have many long years ahead of us – you are so kind and patient and good, maybe you can turn away from sin completely, but I know I would fail.'

'Oh, John,' Basil sighed. 'Don't you know that baptism is one of the ways Christ gives us grace? It shows that we are his, and that even though we'll make mistakes, we're no longer interested in a life lived just for the world and the world's pleasures. If we were to stop sinning completely, how could Paul talk in Romans about his battle against sin? But I firmly believe that, if we commit ourselves fully to him, Christ will give us greater and greater strength to say no to sin. Here's the bottom line: we love Jesus and it's time to tell the world.'

So John and Basil studied yet harder to show the bishop that they understood the Bible and had faith in Jesus, and they were baptised. Yet however much John

---

3. At this time many people thought that it was best not to be baptized until they were dying, because they believed they would be condemned to hell if they committed any sins after baptism. The emperor Constantine the Great, who had only recently died, had a famous deathbed baptism.
4. Hebrews 6:6.

read and prayed and avoided the false, glittering world
of glamorous Antioch, the more he longed to be only
with Jesus. He still had such a long way to go before
his character reflected his beloved Lord. Basil felt the
same way – and had for some time – and soon both
young men reached a decision.

'Mama, I have something important to tell you,'
John said one morning, sitting at the table where his
mother was kneading the day's bread. 'I hope you'll
be pleased. It's something I've been praying about for
a long time.'

'You're marrying a nice Christian girl?' his mother
asked, brightening up.

John recoiled. 'No – the opposite.'

'You're not marrying a pagan!'

'Mama. Listen, Basil and I have been praying about
it for a while, and we want to become monks. We're
going to go live in one of the desert communities and
learn about life with Christ alone.'

His mother leaned back against the wall, crossing
her arms, leaving floury fingerprints on her sleeves.
She couldn't seem to look at him.

'You're not happy?' John faltered.

'I just can't ... I can't believe I have raised such an
ungrateful son.'

'Mama!' John gasped.

'I have had no husband all these years, since your
dear father died. Why? Because I have devoted myself
completely to your Christian upbringing and your

education. And you want to repay me by abandoning me?'

'Of course not!'

'But you propose to go into the desert, far away, where I cannot follow. You will enter poverty and solitude, and at the same time sentence me to poverty and solitude too.'

'But I thought you'd want me to devote myself totally to the teachings of Christ. To repentance. To becoming more like him.'

'Son, you are all I have. You can belong totally to Christ while still living with me. After all, your first duty is to your family. You tell me you want to be a monk; I suppose that means you'll never marry, and I will never have grandchildren.'

'It's a sacrifice for me too. The apostle Paul says there's a blessing on those who don't marry because they can be –'

'–Totally devoted to Christ's work. You don't need to quote it to me. And I can accept that, though it grieves me. But I am asking you not to leave your mother, because I simply couldn't bear it. And if you insist on going, your first act as a monk will be disobeying your parent. Of course, you'll have plenty of time to repent of it.'

John looked down. 'That settles it, then. I will live as holy and set-apart a life as I can without leaving you.'

His mother sighed and dropped onto their other stool. She laid her hands on his arm. 'You would be abandoning your city, too, you know. Antioch could use a preacher with your capabilities.'

'No. I am completely unworthy to serve in such a way. To enter the ministry would bring a judgement on myself.'

'Well, perhaps once you have taken your fill of humility and repentance, you will see that God can use you to preach those things to others.' She held up a finger as John opened his mouth to protest. 'Wait and see how God calls you in the future, son.'

'Yes, Mama.'

'Are you angry with me? It will do me no good having you here if you live in bitterness.'

'No, I'm not angry – just disappointed. I thought I had found what I was supposed to do. It felt like my calling. It still does.'

'Perhaps along with all that humility and repentance you could learn patience,' she said, getting up. 'I won't be here forever. I dare say you will get to live that calling before too many years have passed.'

He looked at her, really looked at her, for the first time in months. As a boy he had thought his young mother the most beautiful woman in the world, and indeed he had seen many men look at her in the same way. Many had wanted to court her, but she had been determined to stay single ever since his father died when he was only a baby – a sacrifice for her son and for her church. She was not old even now, but he could see a worn look in her face, a paleness he'd never noticed before, a slowness in her movements. She didn't look well.

Sudden tears filled John's eyes. Much as he believed that all who followed Jesus belonged to him after death, he loved his mother deeply and the thought of losing her from this world pained him to the core. Now he understood how she felt – if he went away from her now, she would never see him again on this earth. The separation might not be forever, but it would be as long as they lived.

He stood up and kissed her on the cheek. 'Mama, if staying at home for now is a sacrifice, it's one that I make cheerfully. I won't ask to leave you again.'

Losing a Friend,
Gaining a Minister

Although he knew he'd made the right decision, John's feet dragged as he went to see Basil. All those hours they'd spent discussing what it would be like joining one of the tiny communities of monks in the desert, the journey they would make together – well, John felt a bit of a traitor telling Basil he couldn't go, on top of feeling disappointed himself.

'Why the long face, brother?' Basil asked cheerfully when John walked in the door. 'I've been thinking further about the journey out of Antioch. What do you think of Egypt? There's a group of hermits in the Sinai that we –'

John sat down at the table. Despite his inner fight, he made himself look as calm and disciplined as ever. 'I can't go.'

'To Egypt? Well, there are plenty of monks right here in Syria.'

'I can't leave Antioch. It's my mother. She would be all alone in the world. She's begged me to stay and I can't disobey her.'

'Your mother!' Basil flopped into a chair in dismay. 'John, these worldly concerns can't keep us from our calling. We both feel going is the right thing to do. What else can we do to draw closer to God? She can't possibly stand in the way of that. Tell her as a Christian, it's her duty to encourage your closer walk with Christ.'

'Nobody,' John said sternly, 'wants that more than my mother. But perhaps she feels I would be better shaped by obedience here in the city than through solitude in the desert. I can't say whether that's what Christ wants or just what I want, but I do know that he doesn't want me to disobey my mother. She's a follower too, you know – I have to trust that she has some of that wisdom that only comes with following Christ for a long time.'

'Well, say we stayed relatively close to the city ...'

'That wouldn't satisfy either us or her, and you know it.'

As they continued the debate, another friend from their old catechism class came in, breathless. 'Congratulations!' he puffed.

The two men stared at him. 'What do you mean?' Basil asked.

'The deacons are looking for you both. They want to make you bishops[1]. They're on their way here!'

---

1. At this time deacons were the servants of the Church, overseeing practical affairs; priests were preachers; bishops oversaw a number of priests; and really important cities had archbishops who oversaw larger areas. There was no one head of the Church, like a Pope, but archbishops of the most important cities, such as Rome and Constantinople, did have

Basil and John looked at each other. Bishops! For a moment neither could speak.

'We must be united in our response,' Basil said. 'Should we submit to them or run? I don't want them to take us by force as they've done to others who didn't feel ready for the honour. We either agree of our own will, or we both escape. You decide, and I'll follow your inclination.'

John looked at his friend – Basil had not blanched in fear, but blushed in excitement. His eyes were bright, his breathing fast. But John couldn't feel what Basil was feeling. He felt struck by paralysis, his mouth suddenly dry. He had to turn away for a moment as he formed a response.

'They are right to call you, my friend,' John said, turning back. 'You stay here. I'll return to my own home in case they look there first.' He held out a hand and grasped Basil's arm. 'God be with you.'

'And with you,' Basil said. He looked nervous but he was smiling. 'I hope they'll ordain us at the same time. We are true brothers, John, and even more so now that we'll be side by side in ministry.'

John, out on the street, looked around carefully for any church officials, and seeing none, took the darkest and most hidden path away – and not in the direction of home.

---

some unofficial influence over the Church as a whole. The eastern and western churches had not yet separated into Orthodox and Catholic, so there was only one official 'denomination' throughout the whole empire.

He did not see Basil for some days; not until after the ceremony was complete, and John deemed it safe to come out of hiding. It had been a lonely time without much company, missing his friend and wondering what he would say when they met again. And then one morning, not long after John had quietly returned to his mother's house, Basil appeared in his bedroom door as he had so often done during their studies.

'Hello, bishop,' John said, his face splitting into a grin.

Basil didn't answer. He crossed the room and sat in the chair next to John's bed. Even then he seemed unable to speak. His eyes filled with tears.

'It's all right,' John said with a laugh, patting Basil's arm. 'This is exactly what I prayed for.'

'How can you say that?' Basil implored, turning to John. 'Dear friend – I can't even go the marketplace for all that is being said against you. And against me, too. "You must have known John's plan to hide. Why didn't you tell us so we could get you both into ministry?" They say you hid because you're too proud to join the ministry, that you want glory instead of servanthood. I'm too ashamed to tell them you deceived me. What did I ever do to you? Were we not true friends at all?' He held up a hand. 'Don't think I'm coming to accuse you. No doubt whatever you did was right and you had reasons for it. I just want to know what I should tell everyone else.'

John, serious now, nodded. 'Good thing I answer to a higher power, and not to them. Basil, I could see that you were happy to be a bishop, and how could I cheat the Church of such a worthy man? I knew you were called to serve. But I am not, at least not yet. So you had to go before me, and I had to make you. If you knew I wouldn't agree, you wouldn't have either.'

'If either of us was the worthy one, it was you. You're far more talented than I am.'

'At what, law? Debating little points of Scripture? The fact is, you're far more loving and Christlike than I am. What kind of bishop would I be? I say bitter, sarcastic things. I love glory and ambition, and I'm open to the temptation of serving myself, not Christ, from such a position of authority. Besides, I've been baptised for about ten minutes. How could I hope to shepherd old men who actually have experience of the Christian life?'

'But all these are reasons why you should have helped me to escape too! Do you know that when they came to me, they told me that I had to submit, because you already had agreed? They lied to me, and by telling me we should both agree to take up the ministry, you lied to me too.'

'I did what I had to do. I am completely convinced the result is as it should be. You're serving the Church. I still have far more to learn. If Christ ever wants me to lead as a bishop, he will have to finish moulding me first. For me to do it in my current state would be to set myself up for failure, and my church for disgrace.'

'John, you could argue an elephant into becoming a mouse. But there's one thing that really scares me more than anything else. If you, with far more talent than I have, are so unworthy to serve as a bishop, how can I possibly be worthy to serve, and serve well?'

'No one can do this job unless Christ helps him,' John said, laying a hand on his friend's shoulder. 'He will give you all you need to be a good bishop. Basil, I only did what I felt was right.'

'I believe you,' Basil said. 'But I wish we were in it together.'

'We couldn't be more together, my friend. In prayer, we are one, and I'll be praying for you day and night.'[2]

---

2. This entire argument is summarized from a very long essay of John's called 'On the Priesthood', in which he tells the story of tricking his friend Basil when the deacons try to force them into ministry. Some academics believe the story was not from real life, but was a sort of parable John used to explain different things about the calling to Church service.

Leaving Home

The tears, John had decided, belonged back here in Antioch. He couldn't cry for his mother all the way into the desert. He could use that time to meditate on the Scripture by his favourite writer, St Paul: 'We do not grieve as others do who have no hope.'[1] He knew he would see his mother again. He repeated the verse over in his head as he strapped on his sandals for the journey and slid his few scrolls with books of the Bible into his bag. Like the disciples sent out by Jesus, he would take almost nothing for the road, relying on Christians along the way to give him food and shelter.

John had been a monk in his heart for a long while, and now he was finally going into the wilderness he longed for, a life of nature and simplicity, a long way from the temptations of the city, from any kind of luxury. He wanted to find out what Jesus had experienced in his forty days of fasting in the desert. He wanted to sacrifice his every bodily comfort and bring his whole spirit into complete dependence on

1. 1 Thessalonians 4:13.

Christ – for company, for health, for teaching, for life itself when there was no food or heat or medicine.

He stepped out the door for the last time. Off to live the dream.

Goodbye to the rocky street where his mother had wrapped up his skinned knee in linen bandages and kissed it better. Goodbye to the market where she had, on rare occasions, bought him a honey cake and handed it down to him with a secret smile. Goodbye to the doctor's house that he had run to on her last night, before he knew she was really leaving him. How strange it had been, sitting and watching her fight for breath. Seeing her go on ahead to the new land. Trying to imagine her journey to the realm of God himself. She was the one living the dream.

We do not mourn like those without hope, John repeated in his head, but it was too late, his eyes were welling up again. *But we do mourn*, he added. He had come to think of his mother as someone who held him back, but now already he saw how he would miss the way she had smoothed his life, and since John knew he would never marry, he would never have someone again to do that for him. Every step he took through Antioch seemed to bring him some fresh memory of her: the church they'd gone to, a friend's house, a favourite garden. He was glad to get out of the city gate and dry his eyes once more.

He didn't have far to go, but the short distance would bring him to another world. A long day's walk out of Antioch would take him out of sight of the city, away from its gossip and its fashions and its temptations. In the hot Syrian wilderness he would find his destination.

In John's new home there were only a few monks together, all learning from one teacher. They prayed together six times a day, no matter the weather or the darkness. They read the Bible out loud, for the benefit of those who couldn't read. Sometimes tourists or travellers or people looking for truth would make the long journey out to their caves to ask their advice about the Bible or the Christian life or some decision they had to make. And of course they brought news from the city, so the monks weren't completely cut off from the outside world, and they took letters to them or from them. Apart from visitors, there were the little dwellings to keep up, the food to harvest or grind or fish to find. In short, monastery life was a tad too busy for John. After four years, he was ready for the next step.

Being a monk was an extreme lifestyle for many people, but those who were very serious about it often went out on their own as an anchorite – a hermit. John was going to the mountains to be totally by himself. He wanted complete concentration, complete solitude for just him and God.

Few people have ever been alone as John was alone. His mountain was baking hot in the summer, dangerously cold in the winter. He ate almost nothing, so there was little time taken up finding or making food.

There were no extra clothes, no need for a routine like taking a bath or cleaning teeth. There was no one to talk to – it was very difficult to find an anchorite who didn't want to be found, so John saw almost no one. He never went to the shops.

He read his Bible, memorizing whole books of it. He fasted in order to pray more, to sharpen his thinking, and to remind himself of how he depended on God for everything. He went days or weeks without ever lying down. He wrote down some of his thoughts about the Bible and its truth. 'I'm so easily tempted by many things,' John thought. 'If I reduce my body to almost no food or sleep, expose it to great cold and heat, there will be no room to be tempted by worldly things. There will be suffering, but it will defeat sin. In the desert there's no temptation to flirt with women, or drink wine, or spend money on fashionable clothes. I want to show God that he comes before even food and sleep for me.'

Some anchorites could live in the desert for years, but John took things too far. By the time two years were up, his health was ruined. He knew God didn't want him to die yet. There was no choice but to make the long, difficult walk back to Antioch. But John's time alone had taught him some things.

He knew how unnecessary many of the things were that worldly people worried about – money, job promotions, safety, sports, beauty. And he was worried that the Christians who cared too much about these things were nothing but worldly Christians.

And he knew what it was like to live as just him and God. On the road back, too, John walked alone with God, and knew that he always would, no matter how many people were around him.

The First Christmas
in Antioch

It was winter, and all of Antioch was abuzz with excitement over the coming festival. The Church had declared a new holiday: the feast of Christmas. Antioch loved a party, and already people had been getting ready for weeks, thoroughly cleaning and decorating their houses, buying gifts, and getting ready for a party. In fact, the whole city was full of anticipation, not just the Christians. The pagans, those who still worshipped the ancient Roman gods, were busy getting ready for the feast of Saturnalia. There was not much difference between the two groups and their feasts.

Many of the Christians enjoyed the Jewish or pagan ceremonies of their neighbours, and it was not unusual for Christians to go to the synagogues and celebrate Jewish holidays – a custom which the powerful new preacher John said was unbiblical, and condemned through several most irritating sermons. The Christians were relieved that here at last was a holiday that he approved of; he had even produced evidence that Christ had been born on 25th December and not on 6th January, as other churches taught.

So on the 20th of the month, the people went to church looking forward to a nice service talking about joy, the baby in the manger, and then going home to a good dinner and more preparations.

John started off well.

'Many ask why we should celebrate Christ's birth at all. But I say it's an occasion that fills me with greater joy than the other church holidays, for it led to them all. If God did not come down and put on human flesh, becoming a baby, there could have been no Epiphany of the prophets realising he was the Messiah; there could have been no Good Friday of his crucifixion, no Easter of his resurrection, no Pentecost of the Holy Spirit coming to dwell in us. Christmas is a great miracle that we cannot possibly understand, that the God of eternity would put on a human body; that the One who breaks the bonds of death was bound by a baby's swaddling clothes.'

Then the sermon took something of a turn.

'And of course we come here and have Communion, and it's as if we are eating and drinking something of that human body – isn't that a miracle in itself? But you do not prepare for this honour, not even on a great spiritual occasion like Christmas! Isn't it absurd to take so much care over bodily concerns, so that many days before the feast approaches you get your best clothes out of your chests and get them ready, and you buy new shoes, and enjoy lavish dinners, and take thought for many provisions from all quarters ... but take no care for your soul, which is neglected, dirty, squalid, wasted from hunger and unclean?'

The people fidgeted. A few slipped out the door.

'Don't say to me that the five days left before Christmas are not long enough to cleanse that soul. One day is all you need to examine yourself and repent of all that is wrong. If you have stolen, you must restore four times over, like Zaccheus. If you have sinned with your mouth, telling lies and gossiping about each other, you must stop this and use your mouth instead to pray and sing psalms to God. Go and clean and decorate and dress your souls, and come back in five days ready to celebrate Communion, the only true feast.'

Sometimes the people felt that John took things a bit too seriously. But the way he explained Scripture to them was so beautiful that they kept coming to hear him – and they knew that he really cared for them, too, especially the poor and oppressed. They didn't much like it when he told them it was wicked to go to the synagogues, or to the races and theatre – where all kinds of immoral behaviour ran wild – but they knew that John lived what he preached. They remembered the brilliant career that he had given up to follow Christ, and that he had once sat alongside them watching the comedians at the theatre or the horse races at the hippodrome. Jesus was so real to John that he had changed his life completely, and they had to admit there was something beautiful, if solemn, about that change. Anyway, if they didn't much enjoy his preaching against their fun, they *did* enjoy his sermons warning the rich about their selfishness and vanity. One of his most famous stories was that of the expensive luxury of silk, imported from China.

'Ships are built, sailors and pilots engaged, sails spread and the sea crossed, wife and children and home left behind, barbarian lands crossed and the merchant's life exposed to a thousand dangers – why? So that you can have silk to decorate your boots. What could be more mad? Your concern as you walk about the streets is that you should not get your boots muddy and dusty. Will you let your soul get dirty while you are taking such great care of your boots? Boots are made to get dirty! If you can't bear it, take them off and wear them round your neck. You laugh! I am weeping at your foolishness.'[1]

For several years John enjoyed preaching in Antioch. His bishop, Flavian, was a very old man, dignified and kind but not a great preacher, and so he set John in the pulpit of the city's cathedral and let him become God's mouthpiece to the people. They had a happy partnership, John working hard for God's Kingdom as he loved to do, Flavian holding the title and living in the bishop's mansion, which didn't interest John in the slightest. And then, before they realised it, everything changed.

---

1. Both the Christmas sermon and the silk sermon are taken directly from John's actual sermons, many hundreds of which still survive.

Riots in the Street

There was trouble in the streets of Antioch. A bad feeling against the emperor, Theodosius, was brewing. The air smelled of it in the public square, where a large crowd was gathered to hear a proclamation sent by the emperor. They had some idea of the announcement that was coming, and no one was happy about it.

'In view of the costly rebellions in the empire, and of the ten-year anniversary of our blessed emperor's reign,' cried the messenger, 'all the wealthiest cities of Asia will be subject to a special tax …'

As he continued with the details, the square was filled with murmuring, one man to another.

'What does the emperor care for us except for our money?'

'I'm just managing to get by. It's not fair to suddenly have to pay far more tax than I can afford.'

'How will I feed my family if I have to pay more?'

'He'll pretend to be very generous with bread and circuses for the anniversary next year, but he'll take all our money for them now!'

A group of troublemakers from out of town decided to stir things up too: 'I don't know why this great city should stand such treatment. I know we wouldn't take it lying down in our corner of the empire. We'd show the emperor his place!'

The buzz grew into a roar. John, now a famous preacher in the city, stood up and tried to calm the crowd. 'Citizens, think before you do dangerous things. Don't listen to these outsiders who want to rile you up. Do you think they have Antioch's good in mind?'

But it was too late, the people had heard what they wanted to hear – and from the outsiders, not the preacher. They saw their riches dwindling before their eyes and they were too angry to listen to anything else.

The city erupted into violence. Gangs of furious men attacked the public baths[1], destroying the grand building. Those with a bit more sense ran to Bishop Flavian's house to ask him to talk reason into the people, but he wasn't home. The men charged like one person toward the governor's praetorium.[2] They ran into the great judgement hall only to find it empty. 'He's nipped out the back!' they told each other, outraged.

Having expected to vent their anger to the emperor's official representative, they did not know what to do next. As the men scattered along the polished marble

---

1. Since most people didn't have baths in their own homes, the cities' public baths were popular meeting places. They were a bit like big bathtubs and a bit like a spa, and some of them were really magnificent. Anyone could go in and relax there for a small fee.

2. A bit like a courtroom, the governor would give his judgements here.

floor, glancing at each other, they became as still as the bronze statues of the imperial family that lined the circular wall. Should they wait? Come back? Root out the terrified governor? Then a boy stepped forward, and a stone whizzed through the air and clattered against the bronze emperor's head.

The mob broke into a frenzy. They smashed the statues of the emperor and his family and threw them into the street. New riots broke out in different parts of the city, attacking the houses of other officials, pulling down a statue of the old emperor, Theodosius' father. The Antiochans were so furious they didn't stop to think what they expected to achieve with their anger – or what the consequences might be. Imperial officials and their families locked their houses and peeked through the cracks in their window frames, holding their breath, praying the mob wouldn't burst through their door, preparing to flee as soon as there was a calm.

Then the army appeared. Lines of soldiers with blades ran at the crowds or thundered in on horses, stooping from their saddles to cut them down. It was terrifying, each person running for his house, praying he hadn't been identified as one of the mob. With the streets cleared, the stillness of fear fell over the city. The emperor would hear of this rebellion. He was known for his temper, and his power was enormous. He would have his revenge. He would crush them.

In the days to come Antioch could barely breathe. Fear hung over the city like a cloud, wafted its way into every house, could be tasted in every bite of food. Already messengers would be on their way to the imperial city to seal their doom.

'I must go to Constantinople,' Flavian told John. 'I'll go to the emperor and plead for the city, that he might not massacre it. Perhaps God's judgement will still fall on us, perhaps this is the destruction of Antioch, but I must go and intercede for the people.'

'It's the work of Christ, and I know he'll go with you,' John said. 'I'll stay here and talk some sense into the people. If the emperor will be reasonable, he'll find that the city will too.'

'I know you'll bring them round. You can command a city from a pulpit, my friend.'

John was in his forties now, and had been serving Antioch tirelessly as a preacher for years. He had a reputation for speaking powerful truths, just like his hero, the apostle Paul. The poor loved him; the rich didn't love him quite so much, but they still respected his influential voice. Now John had an opportunity to speak and be heard like never before –just as people pray more when they're facing disaster, so the people of Antioch rushed to church to hear John's wisdom and counsel.

'It is fitting,' he preached, 'that we must plead to God for our lives during this particular season of Lent. This is a time when we make a special point of denying ourselves pleasure and luxuries in order to pay greater attention to the things of God. It's a time when we concentrate on repentance and renewing our commitment to God's things. Do you realise that, just as God used Joseph's ordeal in Egypt to save the children of Israel or Paul's imprisonment to save his jailor, he will use this time of hardship and fear to do something good? Often it's only when they're facing punishment that people will change their sinful lives.

'Look at the city: the churches are full and the theatres are empty. Many of you are realising that the circus and horse races can't satisfy you, only the things of God. But this repentance, and seeking God, must last. You can't just go back to your old ways as soon as the danger passes.

'Anyway,' he added, 'if you're really Christians, there's nothing to fear in death. If you believe in Christ, death is nothing more than an unusually long sleep. It's like sailing into a beautiful port after a long, hard journey. Why, you should be ashamed of how you're panicking! Instead of getting the pagan officials to reassure you, you should be impressing them with your Christian courage and peace.'

So the city had nothing to do but wait. Of course there were rumours – the emperor was furious; the emperor was calm; the emperor was sending another army; the emperor was coming himself – and with every new rumour the people went to extremes, piling into churches when fear was high and wandering back to the theatres when things looked more optimistic.

After a few weeks two officers arrived and gave the emperor's verdict. There would be trials for the main culprits, but in the meantime there were immediate consequences. Antioch would no longer be the capital of Syria, for a start. ('What does Antioch care about being the capital of Syria?' John lectured his people. 'We're not dishonoured by our loss of rank, but by our sin. Anyway, our importance is in our history with Paul and Barnabas, and in being the place where people were first called Christians.')

The circus and theatres would be shut. ('No loss there,' said John.)

Even the public baths, the ones that hadn't been destroyed in the riots, would be closed. ('Wash in the river,' said John. 'Mind you, some of you have already been doing that, and I *would* ask that you take a bit more care for your modesty!')

John's somewhat unsympathetic reassurance was not enough to calm the crowds. The poor, who had taken part in the riots, still quaked at every new dispatch from Constantinople. The rich, who would be held accountable, took this last opportunity to disappear.

The trials began, with the threat of heavy punishment hanging over the accused. But they had barely started when John received some reinforcements. The monks from the mountains around Antioch – the very same communities John had lived among years before – streamed into the city, against the tide of the rich who were running away from it. They were so bold that the emperor's officers agreed to listen to their representative, Macedonius.

'Officers, you must return to the emperor and ask him for mercy,' he said. 'How can he take the lives of men made in God's image because they damaged statues made of bronze? He can't get their lives back once they're gone, but he can make as many new statues as he wants. And if he insists on sentencing all these men to death, we monks are ready to give our lives in their place.'

The officers agreed to return to the emperor with the message, and a temporary peace returned to the city. 'Look at the world's teachers and philosophers, with their dignified long beards and cloaks and staffs, advertising their own wisdom,' John said. 'Where are they? In the mountains, hiding in caves. Meanwhile, the monks deserted those caves and came to the city. You can see them walking about the streets as if nothing has happened. You see how Christ frees us from fear? And these poor, humble men, they calmed the storm at once.'

There was more waiting. More rumours. More sermons. And then an express messenger arrived from Constantinople.

The city was pardoned.

Antioch had a holiday. The streets were decorated with lights and wreaths. John's old teacher Libanius, one of the few pagan teachers to stay in the city and pour scorn on the cowards who had run for the hills, delivered heroic speeches celebrating the messenger, the officer who had returned to the emperor, and Theodosius himself. People sang and shouted in the streets. 'May the city remember these lessons it's learned for generations to come,' John said. 'Don't go back to your sin and rebellion just because the time for judgement is over. Remember your bishop standing before the emperor, pleading for mercy on you all for the sake of Christ, who has forgiven not only your sins but the emperor's as well. Remember him standing before Theodosius with his face covered, saying *If you will not send me back with a pardon for them, I won't go back at all.*'

Bishop Flavian finally returned to Antioch, exhausted but victorious, the day before Easter. It was a holiday service with great rejoicing, with all the city understanding better their deliverance from sin by seeing their deliverance from the emperor's just wrath. Thousands of the city's pagans, seeing the courage of the Christians who had interceded with the emperor at the risk of their own lives, became Christians. The riot had led to a revival.

Kidnapped

John found it most encouraging that Astorius, who had authority over a huge region of the empire, had asked him to accompany him to a martyr's memorial outside the city walls. While John didn't have much interest in how important people could help him, he knew very well that people of influence were very useful in leading the common people, and in providing for them too. So he looked forward to the long walk through the city and along the walls, looked forward to the inevitable discussion of the holy man's life and death, looked forward to the challenge he would give Astorius about repentance and renewal.

Astorius seemed in a sober enough mood, but not much interested in the saint under discussion. 'Walking through this city, I see how much good you have done in Antioch,' he said. 'It's a changed place. The Christians aren't taking part in inappropriate Jewish customs. The pagans are less visible. Giving has gone up in our churches – so have numbers. Flavian is a good bishop, but it's down to you, John. People love you and your golden mouth.'

'What rot,' John said. 'I'm nothing. Christ is the one working, he's the one talking, he's the good in it all.'

'And are you satisfied with all you've done on his behalf? Would you be prepared to say your work is through, and label yourself a good and faithful servant?'

'Of course not! How can our work for Christ ever be done until his kingdom has come here on earth? Any good that I've done in this city is next to nothing, compared to the sin and misery I see all around me.'

'Well, I shouldn't worry. No doubt you'll be bishop when Flavian is called up to heaven, and then there's no end to the good you can do.'

John looked at him as if he was crazy. 'You talk as if you know something I don't.'

Astorius simply shook his head and laughed. 'Of the two of us, you should be the prophetic one.'

They passed outside the city gate and Astorius immediately turned toward the martyr's grave.

'I thought you said you'd never been to the site before,' John said, catching up. 'Yet I'm the one following you.'

'I've been once before, but not with an expert.'

John was just about worn out with all the banter by the time they finally got near the grave. The memorial was just in sight when Astorius turned aside toward a carriage and horses standing still by the side of the road. 'Why, what a coincidence – the very carriage that brought me to the city!' he exclaimed. 'Come, John, you must meet the most interesting driver this side of the Bosphorus.'

'I hope he has more spiritual interest than you do,' John muttered under his breath, following his guest.

'May I present the preacher John of Antioch?' Astorius asked, greeting the driver with a wink.

Suddenly two men emerged from the carriage and, before John even had time to shout, they bundled him inside. His eyes had not even adjusted to the dark before they were bumping at speed down the rutted country road. John found his voice.

'What is the meaning of this!' he roared. 'Stop the horses immediately!'

'We cannot,' said Astorius' voice; he must have hopped into the carriage too. 'We must not. It would not do to be delayed at court.'

'At court! What have I to do with court?'

'My dear priest,' Astorius returned laughingly, 'you must know that Constantinople is in need of a new archbishop. I know, of course, that technically the parish of Constantinople is no greater than any of our other big imperial cities – but in terms of influence, this is a promotion beyond your wildest dreams. You will serve the greatest city and the greatest ruler on earth. The emperor himself approved your appointment.'

'I never applied for any appointment!' John protested. 'Haven't I any say in this? I love my city and my people. I believe they love me – they'll be heartbroken.'

'Exactly so,' Astorius agreed. 'That's just why we had to spirit you away. If the people had *seen* us shovel you into a carriage, there would have been demonstrations and bloodshed. We couldn't have more riots in Antioch. Not without you here to calm the crowds!'

'You could have just asked me about taking up a new position.'

'Would you have agreed?'

'Of course not.'

'Well then.'

John hammered a fist against the walls of the carriage. 'Stop this thing at once!' he roared. 'If you take me to the emperor, he will hear of this outrage!'

Astorius laughed. 'The emperor appointed you, you goose. If you refuse, you're the one who'll be punished, not me. You had better try to accept your new job cheerfully. And we're going to be side by side in this cart for a week at least, so you may as well enjoy the journey.'

A New Home

'There it is,' one of the sailors shouted.

Astorius' ears pricked up. He practically jumped to his feet. 'Come and see the city!' he called to John. 'Look – Constantinople!'

'I'm looking at the sea that God made with all its ever-changing hues, teeming with life,' John replied, staring grumpily overboard. 'Why should I leave such a delightful study to consider instead the smoke and chaos of a man-made city?'

'Come on. Get your first look at your new home.'

John sighed and, dragging himself away from the starboard side, lurched over to port.

Even he had to stare.

Constantinople was a forest of pillars, domes, aqueducts, statues, harbours, and absolutely enormous fortified walls. They sailed past the ceremonial city gate with four enormous golden elephants on top, right up the Bosphorus to the royal harbour of Bucoleon. On the far shore, strong men were winding up the huge iron chain that usually guarded the inner reaches of the Golden Horn.[1]

Antioch was an ancient city. It stretched centuries behind that first little band of Christians, into a dim classical past. But Constantinople was new, young, and the roars and bustle, the colours of people dressed in the styles of their own far stretches of the Roman Empire,[2] the gleam of all the new buildings – it was like nothing John had ever seen. His hermit's cave in the desert would be as unimaginable to these streetwise city people as this immense capital would be to a lonely anchorite.

Of the two, John preferred the desert.

Walking off the ship into a marble courtyard – then being escorted through another and another and another marble courtyard, through bright mosaic palace hallways and beneath gold-leafed domes and past dozens of uniformed imperial guards – only served to make him more homesick for his quiet life. Astorius had been replaced somewhere along the route by Eutropius, a tall, skinny old man with a high voice and expensive taste in robes and boots.

'I'm the court chamberlain,' he said with a low bow. 'I don't know if you've heard, but it's actually I who

---

1. Most of the city walls still remain, though they are rundown. The huge iron chain can be seen in the Istanbul Archaeological Museum.
2. The Roman Empire was so large that the emperor Constantine founded Constantinople in A.D. 330 as the capital of the eastern part of the empire. When Rome finally fell, Constantinople would still be going strong in the Eastern Roman Empire. Today, we usually call it the Byzantine Empire.

insisted there was no clergyman in all the empire who could shepherd Constantinople as well as you. The way you handled the Antioch riots – marvellous! We were all so impressed.'

'Ah. So I have you to thank.'

'Well, yes!' Eutropius beamed and waited. John said nothing. 'Anyway, I'll take you to the emperor. We saw your ship arriving, of course, so he stayed back from the Hippodrome to receive you.'

'I'm very pleased to hear that the emperor puts church matters ahead of sport,' John said, relieved that at least someone here seemed to have some real spiritual feeling. 'No doubt his presence is required at the races on occasion, but they're such an unhelpful distraction to one's spiritual life.'

'Oh, they'll make the races wait till he comes, you know. He wouldn't miss them for the world! And there are acrobats to keep the crowd happy till then, so you didn't inconvenience us really.'

While John was still gaping at this assurance, Eutropius asked: 'Do you know much of our new emperor?'

'I spend little time on gossip. I know that Theodosius is dead and his son Arcadius is on the throne.'

'Yes, indeed. You'll be pleased to hear he lacks his father's temper. He also lacks his brains, but between you and me, that makes him wonderfully easy for the right man to influence. At least he's not greedy like his brother. It's said that their tutor retired into the

53

desert to mourn over the wickedness of Honorius and the foolishness of Arcadius. But I, for one, am pleased we have Arcadius – a selfish man won't listen to his advisors, but a stupid man will.' He winked at John.

'One would hope, then,' John said, 'that his advisors at least are wise.'

'Well, some are better than others, of course.'

'Of course.'

They were at a pair of massive doors in a very fancy hallway. 'Ready to meet the boss?' Eutropius asked with a satisfied smile.

'No man is my boss,' John replied. 'I'm sufficiently prepared to meet the emperor.'

Eutropius motioned to one of the imperial guards, who opened the door.

The throne room was filled with more gold and mosaic, with beautiful gold lamps hanging from the ceiling and brightly embroidered couches lining the floor. Against the far wall was a fantastic golden throne with gleaming sculptures of lions and peacocks, and on the throne was seated a majestic figure with flowing purple robes, bright red stockings, boots embroidered with double-headed eagles, and a magnificent jewelled crown. There were jewels everywhere – on the crown, dangling from the crown on silk threads, on his fingers, set in a huge weblike necklace that spread over his whole chest and shoulders. And under the crown was a particularly plain young face with particularly empty eyes. The even more bejewelled empress stood next to the throne like a glittering statue. She was just as beautiful as most women who marry powerful men.

As John walked next to Eutropius, the throne suddenly seemed to lift off the ground. The lions shook their heads and roared; the peacocks sang a tinkling melody. John watched this, surprised but not awed, and made a polite bow as the others in the room fell on their faces. All this for a young man that no one would look at twice in the street if he'd been born a workman or peasant. He needed all these ridiculous trappings to look important.[3]

John waited patiently for the throne to creak back to the patterned marble floor, and then waited for him to speak.

'You may approach to kiss my shoe,' the emperor said in his thin voice.

John stepped forward. '*Basileus*,[4] I am foremost the subject of another Kingdom. I understand I am to work by your side, as the pastor of your court and your capital. I would rather give you the honour due to those whom God has given authority on this earth, and kiss your hand.'

The emperor cast a nervous look at Eutropius, who gave him a nod. 'Very well,' he said, extending his many-ringed hand.

---

3. The throne, which was a wonder of modern hydraulics, was not built for several centuries after Arcadius. However, it helps us to picture the almost unimaginable riches and splendour of Constantinople.
4. This was the Greek title used by Byzantine emperors.

John bent to kiss it. As he stood up, he looked in the emperor's boyish face, his insecure eyes, his limp mouth showing neither the smile of welcome nor the firmness of authority. *And what do you need from your pastor?* John wondered. *What kind of heart beats beneath these heavy silks and treasures?*

The empress coughed slightly, and the emperor brought himself into focus. 'Archbishop, this is the empress, Aelia Eudokia.'

'It is our honour to welcome you to court,' the empress said, with a charming smile. 'We've heard about your skill in calming the crowds. This is something most valuable in this city.'

'Your people are dissatisfied, *Basilissa?*'

She coloured, seeing her mistake. 'Not of themselves, but all the unrest of the empire comes to our door, sir. Outsiders stir up the townsfolk from time to time.'

'A diplomat in the church will be useful,' the chamberlain piped up.

The emperor was frowning at a flaw in his silk robe and scratching at it with his finger.

'*Basileus,* is that the main function you wish me to perform?' John asked. 'To shame your people into obedience?'

'Yes, fine,' Arcadius muttered, still distracted.

'That can be done, most noble emperor. Only I must have freedom to govern the church here in my own way.'

'Of course. Your church, your rules. Keep the peace.' The emperor brightened. 'Is it time for the races now, Eutropius?'

'Yes, *Basileus*.' The chamberlain motioned to a guard. 'Find the archbishop an escort to his residence.'

'Nonsense, Eutropius,' the empress said airily. 'A mere courtier will not do to show the archbishop his home. *You* do it.'

The chamberlain's face fell. 'Yes, of course, *Basilissa*.'

The last thing John heard as he followed Eutropius out of the throne room was the emperor's voice: 'Sorry to miss the acrobats, though. Much more fun than meeting an old monk.'

The walk to the archbishop's residence was a short one. As he passed the front of the Hippodrome with its flags and gleaming horses atop the gates,[5] John could hear the frenzied roar of the Reds and Whites and Greens and Blues all cheering on their team. Crowds of little boys jumped to get a glimpse past the gates at the thundering chariots. Eutropius led John across a white marble courtyard toward a magnificent cathedral. John had heard of the great church of Constantinople. *This must be Hagia Sophia*, he thought.

'An impressive sight, isn't it?' asked Eutropius. He was looking wistfully back at the Hippodrome. John noticed a blue cloth tucked into his belt; no

---

5. The four horses, or quadriga, from the entrance of the Constantinople Hippodrome can now be seen inside St Mark's Basilica, Venice. They were stolen during the Crusades.

doubt his team colour. 'The Hippodrome won't disappoint you. We have the fastest horses, the most exotic animals, the toughest gladiators, and the loudest crowds.'

'What do I care about that?' John asked. 'I'm here to work for the church, not waste my time and the church's money on sport and half-dressed acrobats and the foul language of the crowds. Don't think I don't know what goes on in there. Antioch isn't a backwater, and I wasn't always a monk.'

Eutropius gave a feeble laugh. 'In any case, I'm afraid you won't escape the noise of the Hippodrome, as it's your near neighbour. This is your residence.'

John looked around, bewildered, for something like the small house he'd had in Antioch. Maybe with a couple of bedrooms for junior clergy and visiting preachers; he'd expected that in the capital. But he hadn't expected this. The archbishop's residence, only a few metres from Hagia Sophia, looked not much different to the emperor's own.

'It's a palace,' he said flatly.

'Oh yes, of course. You wouldn't think our archbishopric would be less impressive than any in the world, would you?'

'But why would a simple man of the church need such a building as his home?'

'For the banquets and entertainments, I should think …'

'The what!'

'Not to worry. There's a generous budget allowed for you to host these things. You won't be out of pocket.'

'Me, host banquets! What's next, bringing clowns and dancers in? Unbelievable.'

'Archbishop, you must remember, you're part of the emperor's court now. Almost equal to the emperor himself. A certain…splendour?…is expected. Here, let me introduce you to the housekeeper.' He led John inside the foyer, as huge and pillared and colourful as any in the emperor's palace, and led him up to a lady, simply dressed, but still young and rather gorgeous. John looked at her curiously; her mixture of modesty and beauty reminded him of his mother in her prime, when he had been just a little boy.

'Surely you aren't the housekeeper?' he asked her. 'It wouldn't do to have a woman sleeping under this roof. What would people say?'

'It's all right,' Eutropius butted in. 'Many of the priests here have "spiritual sisters" to keep house for them.'

'They what!' John spluttered.

'If you please, archbishop, I don't live here,' the woman said in a gentle voice. 'I am a deaconess in the convent – it's true we share a wall with the archbishop's palace, but we certainly don't share these quarters at night. I'm well aware of these so-called spiritual sisters, and not one of the women I look after would agree to such a position. We serve with cooking here and with cleaning the city's churches.'

'I'm relieved to hear it,' John said to the woman. 'This house is going to be above suspicion. What is your name?'

'Olympias, sir.'

'Very good, Olympias. I trust we shall be friends, and brother and sister in the truest sense. Now, madam, is there a deacon nearby that I might consult with? Preferably one that was not much favoured by the previous archbishop.'

'Yes, sir, I know just the man. I'll go fetch him from the church – it's only a few steps away – you don't mind waiting?'

'Not at all, my good lady.'

Olympias padded quietly out of the room. Eutropius dug his elbow into John's ribs. 'One of the richest women in the city, that. Shame a bit of it doesn't go on better clothes, though, eh? She could be a looker. Spends it all on the rabble instead – hospitals and gruel and so on.'

'Ah. Well, you have just raised her very much in my opinion.'

Eutropius coughed. 'You know, archbishop, I should be getting back to the palace. No doubt your, erm, deacon will help you get settled in.'

John was busy examining silver vases and candlesticks and chalices inset with painted medallions and rubies. 'Impossible,' he was muttering. 'How much money has been spent on these trinkets?' He straightened up and looked at the courtier. 'Yes, go on back and tell them that my new "home" will be *more than* sufficient for my needs.'

'Shall I tell them you request the entertainment stipend to be stopped?'

'Certainly not! I expect every farthing of income that was awarded to the previous archbishop.'

'Very good, sir.' The chamberlain bowed with some relief. He could understand a priest who wanted to hoard all the riches for himself, but not one who was as uninterested in fashion and colour and fun as this man pretended to be.

'Yes,' John added, more cheerfully, 'think what good we can do for the people of this city with my "entertainment stipend"!'

Eutropius was glad to race back to the emperor's box at the Hippodrome and tell them just what a strange man the new archbishop had turned out to be.

An Introduction to Constantinople

It wasn't long before a bearded young man entered the dining room, ushered in by a male servant. The man came and bowed before John, though he looked a bit startled at his new boss's plain clothes.

'Archbishop, I'm one of your deacons,' he said. 'It's a privilege to meet you, though I confess I'm surprised to have the honour of attending you so quickly. I thought you'd heard I'd had some disagreements with the old archbishop and you were going to put me on silver-polishing duty at the cathedral for the foreseeable future.'

'Oh? Well, I wanted a deacon's opinion,' John said. He gestured at the table in front of him, piled high with cheeses and honeycomb, herbed bread, lamb in a rich sauce, silver pitchers filled with wine, the most delicate fish sauce in a priceless gold cruet, the table decorated with garlands of bright flowers. 'What do you think of my table?'

'Archbishop?'

'I mean, would you say it's too splendid, or not quite splendid enough?'

'It's – impressive, sir.'

'Quite sufficient for one small man! Another opinion if you please – what do you think of my residence?'

'Architecturally, sir, I'm sure it's not behind the imperial palace itself. No doubt such workmanship for the Church does credit to Christ's Kingdom.'

'But we are not in a church. We are in, apparently, my house.'

'Yes, quite,' said the deacon, sounding relieved. 'I've nothing against mosaic and marble – except that there are still poor and sick people in the city, who are used to hearing that the Church hasn't enough funds to care for them. Forgive me, sir, you probably don't want to hear it and you'll banish me out to the suburbs to look after refugee widows, but – but you did ask!'

John finally turned to look at the deacon. He was dressed simply in a belted brown cassock and sandals rather than boots, the plainest of cloaks draped over him, but his face was bright and intelligent, a rosy freshness in his cheeks that made John smile. 'Are you from this city?' he asked. 'You don't look like anyone I've seen in these sophisticated streets.'

'I was once of this city,' the man replied with a boyish shrug. 'Now I have no city except the one above. The former archbishop was of the view that I brought shame on the Church by dressing like a desert monk. "You would not wear a tattered robe to meet the emperor," he used to say, though of course I would, for I have nothing else.'

'I was told you were not a favourite of the former archbishop.'

'We had a difference of opinion. I wanted to see the riches of God's Kingdom scattered among the people, and he wanted to see them on his own table.'

John laughed. 'What's your name, deacon?'

'Serapion, sir.'

'Serapion, does any of this feast appeal to you? You're most welcome to sit and eat if it does.'

Serapion hesitated. 'The former archbishop would never have allowed –'

'I know. But I'm just a simple monk, and you're my brother. Sit with me.'

Serapion sat down. 'Perhaps a little bread, sir. To tell you the truth, I've sworn off meat. It's part of my spiritual discipline.'

'And I couldn't eat it if I tried. Ruined my digestion when I lived in the desert.' John turned in his chair and gestured to the woman standing behind him. 'Olympias?'

'Yes, sir?'

'I have a weak constitution, and besides that I lack the imagination to even guess the price of all this gluttony. From now on we dine on plain bread, vegetables, broths. We'll save enough money to feed half of Constantinople. This alone could feed twenty of the beggars outside our door.' He raised his hands to give the blessing. 'O God, we thank you for these good gifts, and for those we are able to give to others,' John prayed. 'Amen.'

When the men raised their heads, Olympias turned around quickly, folding linen napkins on the bureau. But not before they saw the smile on her face and the happy tears glittering in her eyes.

Serapion smiled. 'Sir, you have a reputation for using wonderful words, but a great many more of them.'

'In preaching, perhaps,' John replied. 'But in prayer I remember the words from Ecclesiastes: "God is in heaven and you are on earth. Therefore let your words be few."[1] Now, Olympias, are there other servants in the house?'

'Oh, yes, sir, there are a dozen deaconesses in the kitchen, working on more delicacies.'

'What a blessed waste of time! I want this table cleared at once, do you understand? And all of those delicacies in the kitchen, too. Take them to the poor outside Hagia Sophia. The beggars, the widows, the lame. Give them the feast of their lives, you and your women.'

'Yes, sir,' Olympias said, bursting out with a delighted laugh. 'May I serve you both your – your broth and bread first?'

'Good lady, I was a monk, subsisting on my own for two years. I'm more than capable of spooning my own soup. Go, go, those beggars are far hungrier than I.'

Olympias ran to the kitchen and returned a minute later with a string of women dressed as simply as herself, each of which gave the archbishop a bow and a dazzling smile as she took one of the silver pots from the table. Out went the succulent stewed lamb, the

---

1. Ecclesiastes 5:2.

grouses, the huge basket of spiced bread, the dates and walnuts and fruit.

'Mind you don't forget the fish sauce,' John called after them. 'Everyone loves fish sauce!'[2] He turned to Serapion. 'Eat, young man.'

'Sir, it's a privilege to be invited, but – I'm so happy I don't think I need any food!'

'There are days to fast, son, and days to keep up your strength. It's up to you, of course, but I've just come off a ship, met an emperor, and fed the hungry in body and spirit. For me this is a day for sustenance.' John spoke around a mouthful of bread. 'Anyway, all the world was out there on the street, I couldn't help but notice them as I came in. I'd wager many were once wealthy and now are poor – actresses grown too old for their profession, rich men's widows whose estates were stolen by the government. Riches are treacherous, I always say. Those beggars are the easy ones to minister to. Much harder will be our work with the rich, you'll see.'

Serapion finally laughed and dipped his bread in the fish sauce. 'If you ask me, your real challenge rests with the religious. How much do you know about your deacons and ministers in this city?'

'Not enough,' John replied. 'Now we've dealt with the poor, tell me about the ones who really need our help.'

---

2. Garum, or fermented fish sauce, was the tomato sauce of the Roman world, available on every dinner table. It was made by leaving fish innards to rot in the sun and then liquefying them. Hungry?

The Archbishop's Staff

'O Lord, you have promised to reward your faithful servants,' John prayed. 'Make us worthy of this bounty you have placed before us.'

The city's deacons and priests took their seats at the table, each of them stealing an astonished glance or a quiet smile at the man next to him. Was this plain fare some sort of Antioch tradition, maybe as a first course? Or perhaps John of Antioch simply didn't know how to host a banquet? There were no garlands, no silver plates, no meat. Water instead of wine, plain dry bread with only the most basic garum. Vegetable soup! That was not the main course that fed men such as these, *important* men. And where was the entertainment? Not even a harp player or a singer appeared.

Conversations around the table turned to great dinners that the preachers had been to at the homes of the Constantinople aristocrats, and the latest dishes to appear on the emperor's table, and even the roasted quails or broiled fish they ate at their own homes, cooked by their housekeepers.

John ate a few bites in silence, long enough to get an idea of what the others were talking about. Then he stood and waited. The conversation died down and the men looked up expectantly.

'Brothers, thank you for coming to welcome me to this city,' said John. 'I see that you are all dressed with the dignity your offices require. Even the deacons have embroidered boots and lovely sashes, and as for you bishops! You're gorgeous! All those colours, all those beads and feathers. You, brother, your hat alone could feed a family for a week!'

The priests laughed, feeling more at ease now.

'I see you've all noticed the contents of my table, and are reminiscing about other memorable suppers you have had. I heard that some of you have enjoyed seeing musicians and actresses at some of those soirées. Well, I want to tell you all about one of the most memorable meals I've been party to, with my admirable new friend Serapion here. There were actresses at that one too.'

The men leaned back now, grinning, ready for an exciting tale. They stopped smiling when John described all the deaconesses parading out of the palace with huge platters of food. They stared at the table when he passed on Olympias' description of the filthy, toothless, starving actress in her rags, still raving about her days of glory when even the emperor had thrown her coins, shoving food in her mouth as if she hadn't eaten in days. And as John finished his speech, they went beet red with anger.

'And so I did what I'm sure you have all already done – I gave instructions to my cooks that they should furnish me daily with such food as you have before you now, and spend the rest of the kitchen budget on feeding the poor. That is, of course, on days when I am not fasting; however, on those days there will be more for my deacons to distribute to the poor, so my loss is their gain.'

A stony silence fell over the room.

'Are any of you from outside the city?' John asked. 'Any from a long distance away?'

A few of them stood up.

'Very good. Have you been here long?'

'Two or three months.' 'Six months.' 'A year or so.'

'Oh yes, I've heard of some of you. Severius, isn't it? You have a reputation as an excellent preacher. Are the people in your host church giving generously for the honour of having you with them?'

'Yes, Archbishop. Most generously. It's very good for the Constantinople church coffers.'

John nodded. 'And what of your own church, a week's journey away?'

'I haven't left it unattended,' Severius said defensively. 'I have a good deacon looking after it. He preaches when I'm away.' The other out-of-towners nodded vigorously.

John leaned down with his hands on the table and looked sternly at each of the men. 'Back to your churches that you were called to serve. That is an order. If you are

71

really such wonderful preachers, they are the ones who should benefit. But bear in mind that their eternal good comes not from a preacher with a beautiful tongue, but one with a spirit that honours Christ.'

Those men sat down stiffly. They could not meet anyone's eye now. The other priests were looking quite smug.

'Now,' John said. 'Who has a housekeeper? A woman housekeeper?'

Several of the men stood up nervously.

'We call them spiritual sisters,' one of them spoke up. 'They help us in the work. We couldn't do all we do without someone to keep house and cook.'

'The menservants of my household do those things as unto the Lord, and the deaconesses do it without needing their quarters alongside mine,' John replied. 'I have heard about your so-called sisters. Some of those women know all about church affairs that are private, because you talk to them at night. They gossip to each other so that secret struggles and official church business become common talk in the streets. And then there is the small matter that some of you have had children with these women. *Children!* And you dare to pretend they, and you, are pure servants of the church. There will be no more women, other than mothers and such close relatives, living with any church officer.'

'You have been here a few days,' one of them returned. 'You summon us here for bread and water and give us rules we have never been burdened with.'

'Except by the Lord you claim to serve!' John exclaimed. 'Now. Those of you who wish to live according to Christ's example and to further his Kingdom and serve those in need, you will find me a faithful and kind and affectionate friend. But if I see sin, I dare not tolerate it. Sin brings God's judgement. I will see repentance for these matters, or I will see you out of your churches. This is for the good of your souls, your churches, and this city. Shame on those of you who have harmed the Church by this behaviour. Now you understand me, and if you wish, you may depart to consider these things. Those who want to stay will always find this house and table open to them.'

Many of the deacons and bishops walked out, grumbling as they passed the archbishop.

'Who does he think he is, this monk?' Severius muttered.

His friend replied roughly, 'I'll season his soup for him.'

John and the Heretics

It was dawn on his first Sunday in his new job. John was at his prayers, enjoying the one time of day when the centre of Constantinople was quiet enough to hear birdsong, when he heard a song of a different sort. Going to his window, he saw a large procession of people swaying slowly through the square, holding paintings of Jesus and Mary and singing hymns as they went. John smiled. At last! True Christians in this city! Then he heard the words of the hymns.

Not one with God was the Christ
When Creation was begun;
But born divine from Mary's womb
And now with God is one.

John's mouth tightened in anger. This was not a gleam of spiritual life, but yet another whiff of rot. He stalked out to find Serapion, who had already arrived to accompany him to his new church.

'Serapion, what is the meaning of that unholy procession out there?'

'Arians,' Serapion replied in disgust. 'They believe that Jesus was born a man and was only "promoted" to being God once he'd proved himself. They've been condemned by every church council we've had, of course. Now they're only allowed to have services outside the city — so they spread their evil doctrines by singing them in the streets on their way to the city walls.'

'And this is allowed? This way they force others to listen to them, rather than just meeting by themselves.'

'It's more that nobody wants to be responsible for stopping them. Could turn violent. Especially since most of the Goths, including the imperial guard, are Arians too — no one wants to pull foreigners and soldiers into a civic matter.'

'There must be a way,' John muttered. 'The people of this city seem worldly enough without receiving wrong teaching on top of it.'

'Forget it for now, Archbishop. It's time to get to church. The whole city will be there this morning — for once, everyone's attention will be on the Word of God.'

Along with all his other deacons, John walked to Hagia Sophia, the magnificent pillared church right across the square from the imperial palace. The church was crammed full of people all jostling to get a first look at the new archbishop. The city was already full of gossip about how he had treated the deacons and bishops. A man who could do that must be arrogant. There was no official robe or uniform for the archbishop, so he could be as grand as he liked. They craned their necks for a view of a preacher in gorgeous robes. They half expected the new priest to come sauntering in at the emperor's side.

When the emperor and his family and courtiers had filed in and were sitting in their place – the only ones sitting in a church that was standing-room-only – a little figure that no one had even noticed ascended the steps of the carved marble pulpit: skinny, with a wispy brown beard and a big bald forehead. He was dressed as a monk in a tunic, clean but almost offensively plain. His voice too was thin and reedy, and the people had to keep silent to hear him.

'I woke this morning to the sound of singing,' he told them. 'Like so many things, it was beautiful on the outside, but wicked in its message. Are you all not ashamed of your city, that you allow these heretics to parade through your streets every week, forcing everyone to hear their lies about our dear Lord? I am told that you are all afraid of the reaction of the Goths who belong to their faction. Here's what I want to do to those savages.' He leaned forward.

'I want to send missionaries to teach them more clearly the truths of Scripture. How are they to know any better? They've never heard the truth. I am calling for preachers who can speak their own language to go out there and teach, and I will do it myself if someone will interpret. We will send missionaries throughout the empire to teach these Goths the way of Christ, and they in turn will spread his Word throughout their own lands.

'You wealthy aristocrats – there are many of you here today – I appeal to you. How can you come here with your boots all tricked out with elaborate silk designs, so that you fear to even step in the mud lest you get them dirty, and know that the barbarians on our very doorstep are dying in darkness of soul? I need your funds, not for entertaining visiting preachers or beautifying the archbishop's palace, but for building hospitals and feeding the hungry and reaching the lost. If you see the suffering all around you and look away, I will not hold you blameless.

'As for those who hold these shameful Arian views and spread them so easily, they know very well that their doctrines are wrong and have been condemned by every right-thinking Christian. So I call on you all to walk alongside them in the weeks to come, not hassling or striking them, but singing even louder. Drown out their lies with the truths of Scripture. Do not allow the glory of Christ to be sullied in these streets without even a word of protest.'

Soon the city blazed with talk of John of Antioch, his forceful challenges, his beautiful explanations of Scripture and, more than anything, his despising of the rich and powerful who oppressed the poor. In his first year in Constantinople, he saved enough money from his 'entertainment stipend' to build a new hospital for the poor. He sent missionaries and preached to the Goths himself, using an interpreter. The Arian processions were banned after their members clashed with John's followers, so that several people died – not exactly what John had planned, but there were no more lies about Christ being sung in the streets. He also told off the common people for spending too much time and money at the races, but they loved him so much they forgave him for that.

The rich – they were not so quick to forgive.

Enemies in the Palace

John's visits at court had become awkward. The empress Eudokia was furious again, her fists clenched as she rebuked him for some criticisms he'd levelled against certain wealthy ladies. 'How dare you speak out against those three women! You know perfectly well they're my closest friends!'

John gave a nod. 'They are not worthy of the company they keep, empress.'

'That is hardly your judgement to make, Archbishop. You are here as a spiritual adviser, not to interfere in court life.'

'Madam, if I see court ladies behaving in an immoral fashion, corrupting others to do the same, and cheating the poor, it falls under my spiritual jurisdiction. I would not have this palace fall into disrepute because a few of the widowed ladies-in-waiting cannot conduct themselves appropriately.'

'Be reasonable,' said Eutropius the chamberlain. 'You can't expect the same standards from court women that you do from your widows who have dedicated themselves to church affairs.'

'I can expect the standards of decency,' John shot back. 'The whole city gossips about what the court does. And if they see those ladies carrying on with lords' – here he gave a meaningful look to the empress, who blushed –'and cheating people out of their money, that's the example they want to follow.'

'My friends and I don't need you to defend us, Chamberlain,' Eudokia told Eutropius hotly. 'And you, John, you are the one who has damaged our reputations, with your pronouncements –'

'Madam, I did no such thing. I spoke to those ladies directly. I hardly addressed them from the pulpit!'

'– and I demand that there shall be no further judging of my friends, or we shall have to – to – husband, I wish you would speak up, instead of just letting me defend the entire palace to this monk!'

'Yes, quite right, dear,' Arcadius muttered. He'd been sitting there the whole time, staring at some official letter. 'What does "municipal" mean again?'

'It means "belonging to the city", *Basileus,*[1]' said Eutropius, with the patient air of a man who had explained this many times before. He turned back to John. 'Have you forgotten all the gifts that these wealthy widows have given to the church?'

'And me?' Eudokia added. 'All the pilgrimages I've made to the shrines, and all my donations to the poor.'

---

1. The Byzantine way to address the emperor, as we would say 'Your Majesty'.

'One would hate for that money to disappear overnight.'

John looked from one to the other of them and shook his head in disappointment. 'Always your first and last thought, Eutropius. How many times have I warned you that riches will betray you? I've met too many people in this city who were once rich as you, and now are beggars on the streets. Don't build your hopes on wealth.

'*Basilissa*, I do not wish to pick a quarrel with you. I have indeed seen you to be religious. But as your pastor I counsel you to take care, and understand that religion is not the same as being a follower of God. And it is not the size of your donations that makes the difference, but the object of your faith.'

'You may go now,' Eudokia snapped.

'I'll see you out,' Eutropius added, as John gave his usual slight bow. In the hallway, he murmured, 'Archbishop, I have a very slight request to make of you.'

'What is it now?' John said wearily.

'You have this practice of allowing criminals to take sanctuary in the church.'

'You mean that when you try to have your enemies arrested on exaggerated charges, I allow them safety at the altar? Yes, I admit it, sir.'

Eutropius flushed angrily. 'It is not your judgement to make. If I give orders for an arrest, it's for a good reason.'

'Yes, usually someone has refused you some kind of dignity or donation and you've decided that's grounds to throw them in prison or exile them altogether. Don't forget I am a member of this court. I am not blind to what happens.'

'Then you will not forego your protection of known law-breakers? That makes you an enemy of the emperor in whose name these arrests are made.'

'I am no man's enemy. But I will not deliver innocent victims to you. Sanctuary is a principle from God's law, handed down at Mount Sinai. It will long outlast me – and you.'

'I am in a position to make a considerable donation to the church in exchange for your help.'

'Dirty money! If I were to accept such a thing, my conscience would torment me till I went to scatter it in the potter's field.'[2]

Eutropius' face became a mask of rage. 'Don't you know that Arcadius is about to make me Consul? My power will be second to only the emperor himself! I will destroy you.'

John looked down and smiled before meeting Eutropius' eyes. 'Is it you who is blind? I am in no man's power and never could be, any more than Christ was in men's power when he was sent to the Cross. And you, you who started out as a slave boy to Roman soldiers, you who did their dirty work, you who climbed to the

---

2. This is what Judas Iscariot did with the silver pieces he'd received for betraying Jesus, before killing himself.

lofty heights of Consul by means of greed and trickery and corruption – see that those you have used as stepping-stones do not trample you underfoot.'

'You fool, I'm the one who brought you here!' Eutropius snapped. 'Archbishop of Constantinople, all because of me! Why do you hate me so?'

'Those who flatter and indulge and use you, those are the ones that hate you,' John told me. 'But I, and my church, we love you. We love you enough to tell you the truth.'

Days later, an imperial messenger arrived at the archbishop's house first thing in the morning. 'From the *basileus*, Archbishop,' the young man said, bowing as he handed over a sealed parchment.

John opened it.

Let it be known that the emperor Arcadius by imperial decree has ended the practice of sanctuary. Any person running from justice who takes refuge in any church must henceforth be surrendered to officers of the law.

'Thank you,' said John. 'I have received my instructions and I know exactly what to do next time some poor soul claims sanctuary.'

The messenger bowed and left, and John crumpled the parchment and threw it on the floor for one of the servants to burn with the rest of the trash.

* * *

John loved the emptiness of Hagia Sophia at dawn, long before the congregation arrived, when it was only his own and one or two deacons' footsteps that echoed through the marble walls, the vast darkness lit only by candles and oil lamps. This was God's house, and the splendour of this building did not seem out of place as it did in the archbishop's residence. John needed little sleep, and he preferred to be here when he could, just a few dozen metres from the palace which was supposed to be his home but felt more like a prison.

The early morning silence was broken by a desperate hammering at the church doors. John looked up, not entirely surprised. This had happened before. 'Perhaps another poor soul needing sanctuary,' he said. 'Serapion, go and see, will you?'

Serapion went to the door. As he opened it a familiar voice, shouting in panic, filled the church. 'Finally! Thank you, brother. For pity's sake let me to the altar – they're after me!'

And the new consul, Eutropius, ran across the church, his polished boots sliding on the marble so that he fell, but he scrabbled to his feet and collapsed panting before the altar on which the bread and wine were laid for Communion.

John sat down next to him and quietly waited for the courtier to get his breath again.

'It's that barbarian's doing,' he finally gasped, 'the one that led the revolt. All his threats scared the emperor. And his condition for peace was my removal. The emperor ordered my arrest. That fool Arcadius, after all I've done for him – the empress too, who owes her position to me – they've all betrayed me.'

'But how can I help you? You removed the right of sanctuary,' John asked.

Eutropius' eyes went wide and wild. 'You would use that against me, wouldn't you! Just to spite me! Look, when I get my wealth back, when the emperor sees his mistake –'

John shook his head. 'That is all gone, my friend. You know that. But you may make this altar your safety as long as you wish, law or no law.'

He got up to return to his duties, but Eutropius grabbed the bottom of his tunic. 'Archbishop! They will get in here. Those hounds, those dogs, they were at my very feet. They'll burst in the doors any moment.'

John gently took his hand away. 'They never dared before, and they won't now. I defend my church with my life, and I will defend you just the same. Didn't I tell you it's the Church that truly loves you, Eutropius? Now is the time to repent. This altar is your safety in life. Make Christ your safety for death.'

He went back to the vestry and started looking through his scrolls. 'Are you changing your sermon, Archbishop?' Serapion asked.

'Yes, my friend. I think Ecclesiastes is a more fitting address this morning.'

A huge clamour arose at the doors of Hagia Sophia, men's angry shouts and staffs beating on the wood. Eutropius screamed.

'It's the imperial guard,' John remarked. 'Serapion, wait here with the refugee. I'll be back in a moment.'

He went to the door and opened it to find dozens of soldiers with furious faces. 'Let us in,' their captain said. 'We have an imperial summons for the consul's arrest and you know the right of sanctuary has been overturned.'

'My good men,' John said, 'you are trying to do your duty and arrest a wicked man. I commend you for it, but to do so in the church is impossible. You come in only over my body.'

'That can be arranged,' said one of them, raising his heavy rod.

John put up his hands. 'I appeal to the emperor. You do not have his authority to strike the archbishop. Take me to him and allow him to decide between us.'

A Special Audience for a Special Sermon

There was barely room to breathe in Hagia Sophia when John arrived back from the palace. The usual pickpockets were having the time of their lives in the overcrowded church, but everyone else's attention was completely trained on the trembling figure trying to hide behind the altar. John gave him a nod to let him know it was all right: the emperor had agreed that the church would again give sanctuary. What a strange sight Eutropius was, still in his court robes and boots, but stripped bare of any dignity. The common people screamed insults at him; it was clear that, had he not been in the church, they would have thrown rocks as well as words at the man who had cheated so many.

Even when John went to quiet the congregation for the sermon to begin, there was a buzz rolling through the people, a frisson of simmering fury against the villain at the front.

'Vanity of vanities, all is vanity,' John began, preaching from Ecclesiastes 1, and the people gave a cheer of triumph. Vanity – all for nothing. All for nothing, that wicked man's plots and greed. John waited for the furore to die down and continued, directly facing the consul.

'It is always a good time to be reminded of this, but more especially now. Where are the brilliant surroundings of your high office? Where are the gleaming torches? Where is the dancing, and the banquets and the festivals? Where are the flower garlands and the curtains of the theatre? Where is the applause which greeted you in the city, where the cheers in the Hippodrome and the flatterings of the spectators? They are gone, all gone. Where are your pretend friends? Where are your drinking parties and your suppers? Where are the wine which used to be poured all day long and the dainty dishes invented by your cooks? Where are those who did and said everything they could think of to win your favour? They were all dreams which have vanished with the dawn, bubbles which have burst. Look at this man. His face is like a dead man. His teeth are chattering. He's a petrified soul.

'Now I don't say these things to insult his misfortune, but to soften your hearts toward him. Be content with the punishment he's already received. There are those of you who have come here to stare at him, and at the same time say I shouldn't have even given him sanctuary. Brothers, let's glorify God for permitting this man to be placed in such a terrible position in order to drive him to the Church, and let's show him our power and love. We are the servants of the crucified One who said "Forgive them, for they know not what they do." And this man, who has cheated so many of you and has had the cheek to come here and claim sanctuary even after robbing others of this right, speaks to us a silent warning: "Don't do what I have done, lest you suffer what I am suffering."

'Remember that since he came here, even the emperor has tried to allay the wrath of the soldiers, declaring that he is thankful for all the good this man has done, along with his evil works. If even the emperor has forgiven this person who has cheated him, why should you be so furious when you have not been insulted yourselves? How can you take Communion after calling for his death? How can you pray this prayer, "Forgive us our debts as we have forgiven our debtors?"'

The people were in tears and grey-faced with shame. They could not even stare at Eutropius as they went up for Communion, and there was no heckling as they quietly filed out of the church.

When the church was finally empty again, John sat down wearily by Eutropius. 'I think you have no more to fear from the people of this city, at least. Those who were baying for your blood yesterday in the Hippodrome leave chastened from the church. When will you learn we are your true friends here? You think we've opposed you, but we only opposed the wicked things you did that got you into so much trouble. I always had your good at heart.'

'Well, you may have turned away the people's wrath for the moment, but they are hardly going to protect me from that pack of soldiers,' Eutropius replied, pulling his knees up tight to his chest.

'Your security is with God now – and the Church – not with man ,' John replied. 'As long as you stay here you're safe.'

'I can't stay here forever!'

'Perhaps the emperor will change his mind as to your punishment in time. But you must be patient and wait until it's safe. Until then, you have plenty of time to meditate on all those sermons that you heard here – or pretended to hear, while staring at all the new fashions and listening to the court's witty remarks. Feel free to read my scrolls of the Scriptures while you're in here. I recommend Paul, he's my favourite.'

'You're not going to leave me alone in here all night, are you?'

'God will be with you,' John said. 'And may you open your heart to know his presence.'

John went about his business in the next few days, visiting the poor, preparing his sermons and giving instructions on building a new hospital. Once in a while he stopped into Hagia Sophia to try and calm down Eutropius. It seemed to do little good, and yet every time he left again, Eutropius cried and clung to him, begging him not to go.

Late in the week, the deacon on duty in the great church, Cassian, shook John awake. 'Archbishop,' he whispered urgently. 'It's Eutropius.'

'What about him?' John asked, at once alert. He'd slept lightly ever since his days in the desert.

'He's gone.'

'How? Was the church invaded?'

'No. I went to see him after going about my duties in the vestry. He wasn't there. I searched the whole church, calling him. It was empty.'

'He's run away,' John murmured. 'And there is nothing we can do to protect him now.'

'He might have got away. He must have had a plan, he wouldn't have just run blind.'

But by morning, the streets were filled with chatter. The great consul Eutropius, that terrified, shrunken spider they'd seen clinging to the Hagia Sophia altar, that infamous cheat and liar, was facing justice. He'd run from the church practically into the arms of the soldiers stationed outside. Those who had been willing to show him mercy inside the confines of the great church were less interested in showing grace to the captured criminal.

The woman Eutropius had chosen as empress was ruthless in calling for his blood; the man he had chosen as an unwilling archbishop pleaded for mercy. A few months later, the second most important man in all the empire was beheaded.

The Tall Brothers

There was little rest after the drama of Eutropius. Constantinople thrived on scandal, gossiping equally about the palace and the Church, and even the deepest questions about Scripture were hotly debated in the streets and the Senate. So it wasn't long before they were looking for the next scandal.

The start of it seemed innocent enough, as Serapion introduced some visitors to John.

'Archbishop, these are three monks from Egypt who have come to ask for your help, and a bishop who travels with them,' he said.

Three men who looked like very thin giants stepped forward. They still seemed covered with the dust of their desert, wearing their ragged cloaks, and had clearly made no effort to clean themselves up before meeting the archbishop. John liked them at once. With them was an extremely old man who introduced himself as the former bishop Isidore.

'Welcome to Constantinople,' John said. 'Can I offer you some bread and fish sauce? Perhaps some soup?'

The brothers exchanged a pleased look. 'We heard you were a man to offer us plain things we could eat, not fancy food and entertainment,' one of them said.

'How refreshing after the archbishop we've left behind!' added the second.

The third held up his hand. 'Let us introduce ourselves before we sit down to food. Archbishop, we are known as the Tall Brothers. For years we have lived together in peace in the desert, spoken with any who come to us for advice, and written a number of books and essays on our beliefs. We used to be priests and deacons in Alexandria, until we understood that our archbishop, Theophilus, was a greedy and ambitious man, and no true man of God at all.'

'A rascal!' exclaimed the second.

'A disgrace to the church!'

The third brother waved at them to be silent. 'Peace, brothers. Sir, this bishop in wolf's clothing has recently decided to pick a fight with us, because we sheltered this man from him.'

'Ah yes,' John said, nodding at the old fellow. 'I have a feeling I've heard before of Isidore of Alexandria.'

Isidore made a slight bow, as much as his bent old frame could manage. 'Theophilus proposed me for your position, Archbishop. He wanted to have the head of Constantinople's church, with the emperor's ear, under his power and influence. He thought I was a silly old fool who would do whatever he wanted.'

'I take it you proved him wrong.'

'Last year a wealthy widow gave me some money to buy clothes for the poor. She ordered me not to let Theophilus know, for she realised he was a greedy soul. Well, he found out about it and demanded I give it to him. When I refused, he accused me of a dreadful sin and made it known in the streets, so that I had to run away from the city.'

'He ran to us,' said a Tall Brother.

'We are old friends,' added the second.

'We took him in gladly,' said the third. 'But when Theophilus found out Isidore was with us, he took away our ministries in the church and threw me into jail.'

'And we invaded the jail and sat there with him until he was forced to throw us all out!' the second added delightedly.

'And we went back to our desert home,' said the first. 'But not for long.'

'That vile man came upon us by night with all the coarsest people of the city, in a mob,' Isidore said, shivering at the memory. 'He burned our cells and our books. The other monks, hundreds of them, tried to fight back, but they were driven out.'

'All of our brothers, where are they now?' mourned a Tall Brother.

'Friends,' John said, 'He accused you of nothing but taking in a man running from an accusation of sin?'

'No, he came up with something else,' said the second Tall Brother. 'You are aware, of course, of the writings of Origen.'[1]

John nodded, stroking his beard. 'I have read some of them. Origen has been particularly controversial lately. Some very powerful men in the Church have condemned him, right up to the Archbishop of Rome.'

'We are the reason why,' said the third Brother. 'Theophilus knew that we have based our writings on Origen, so in order to have a reason to go after us, he declared that we, and all who follow Origen's writings, are heretics.'

'Even though he himself is known to be a devoted reader of Origen.'

'And he knew we would come here, so he sent one of his bishops ahead to slander us in the streets.'

'We ask you to call Theophilus to account and defend our honour as Christians.'

This time it was John who silenced them with a hand. 'Brothers, this is a very serious accusation against your archbishop. And if it all happened in Egypt, I can't interfere – I have no authority there, and Theophilus will be even more furious if I meddle. So you must not preach in the city, and you will not stay here with me, but you may stay at another of our church residences. It must not appear that I am giving you my approval without hearing Theophilus' side of the story.'

---

1. Origen was one of the most important writers of the early church. He saw layers and layers of complicated symbolism in the Bible.

'There's more,' said the third monk. 'He's claiming you're an Origenist as well, since you haven't joined everyone else in condemning all his writings. He's trying to destroy your authority and making out that you're a heretic too.'

'But I have no real interest in Origen at all,' John exclaimed, driving his right index finger into his left hand. 'There's good and bad in his writings, as there is in almost anyone outside of Scripture. He "interprets" a bit too much about the Bible for my taste. But there's not much danger to me if they can't find his influence in my sermons, which they won't. My approach to the Bible is much more straightforward.'

'You underestimate Theophilus,' Isidore said, shaking his head. 'He's never forgiven you for becoming archbishop instead of me – though I myself am very glad of it. Theophilus never forgets a grudge and he'll do anything for revenge. He has no idea of loyalty either, and he is a stranger to truthfulness. Beware of that man's fury.'

'It's a shame that he should bear a grudge against me when I did not even want the job!' John laughed. 'Well, if that's how it is, it's particularly important that I'm not seen to interfere. But I do have a suggestion. If you're determined to see justice done, you might want to go to another authority, one Theophilus won't dare to fight.'

'Who?'

'The empress will pass through the streets this week on her return from the summer palace. She is a religious, or perhaps one might say a superstitious, lady who craves the prayers of holy men. If she will take on your cause, the emperor himself can summon Theophilus to a trial here in Constantinople. This is the proper place for a trial, if you have been slandered here, but it's better the emperor tells him that rather than me.'

'We will take your advice, brother.'

'Thank you for your help and refuge.'

'And God's blessing be with you.'

'And also with you, brothers,' John said. 'May you get back to your desert soon to continue your worship and writing.'

Theophilus Turns the Tables

The empress listened to the Tall Brothers' request and asked her husband to bring the Archbishop of Alexandria to Constantinople to stand trial. He obeyed the emperor's summons – after a fashion. He made his journey from Egypt to Constantinople something of a pleasure trip, stopping at friends' mansions, picking up supporters along the way. 'The emperor needs me in the capital,' he told them. 'Apparently there's some small matter that that Origen-loving heretic – that monk living in the archbishop's palace – that *John of Antioch* – cooked up. Something about slandering some unimportant desert-dwellers. Someone should put that impostor of an archbishop in his place. I'm simply exhausted with travel. Yes, another cup of wine would be most helpful to restore my spirits.'

It was many months before he finally arrived in Constantinople. When he arrived, Serapion was waiting for him at the harbour. 'Archbishop Theophilus, sir,' he said, 'I bring greetings from the Archbishop John. He bids you welcome to

Constantinople and invites you as his brother to stay with him in the ecclesiastical palace.'

Theophilus looked down coldly at this humble deacon who dared to address him directly. 'No thank you.'

'Then perhaps you can name a time when it would be convenient to meet with John and bring him tidings from Alexandria.'

'No need.'

'At any rate, sir, do please worship with us in Hagia Sophia this Sunday.'

'I will not.'

Serapion looked confused. 'May I give him a message, sir? Saying why?'

'No message.'

Theophilus swept past the deacon and into a waiting litter[1].

* * *

'And I saw them head off toward Pera,' Serapion said later, telling John what had happened. 'I tell you, John, that man wants something, and it sounds very much like it's your head on a platter.'

'I should be so honoured, as to die like John the Baptist,' John cheerfully replied. 'Seriously, Serapion, there is nothing he can charge me with, and he's in my city now, not I in his. But if there is some kind of argument between us, I will not allow any impression

---

1. This is a bit like a fancy stretcher which people would use to carry important people through the streets.

that it's coming from my side. We will write him a courteous letter repeating the invitation and deliver it to him wherever's he's staying. That's what Christ does for us: he invites us over and over again to come to him.'

But it was hard to ignore the game that Theophilus was playing. At least, it was for all who loved John – his deacons and priests and the people in his churches. John himself seemed almost unaware of the whole drama, going about his normal business of preaching and counselling and directing the missions and the donations to the poor. However, his followers could talk of little else but what was happening in Pera. Finally, some of his priests and deacons got John's attention long enough to explain what was happening.

'Theophilus has gathered together all those bishops that you sent back to their own churches, and those whom you forbade to have spiritual sisters, and those that wanted easy living instead of looking after the poor.'

'He's being constantly visited by all the rich folks who have taken offence at your preaching against their corruption and luxury and immoral behaviour.'

'And he's encouraging all that corruption and luxury and immoral behaviour. He's doing everything you refused to do – throwing banquets, giving expensive gifts, flattering everyone around him.'

'Those widows, the friends of the empress that you offended, are helping gather people to Theophilus. Their gossip and slander is outrageous and those who want to believe it do believe it.'

'He sent some monk called Isaac to Antioch to try and find any sin from your youth that they can use against you.'

'Worst of all, he's moving his base from Pera, just across the Golden Horn, to a house called The Oak in Chalcedon. He knows there will be riots in the city when they make a formal accusation against you, and he wants to be well away from any danger.'

John listened to all this calmly. 'But you forget he himself has been brought here to answer charges. He is still awaiting his trial.'

'John,' said a priest, Tigrius, 'no one has come forward to accuse him. You insist it's not your place to do so, and the emperor simply hasn't laid any charge – he thinks it's a church matter. And the men who actually spread the slander against the Tall Brothers have already been punished, so Theophilus is behaving as if the whole thing is already over. And I think perhaps it is.'

'Brothers,' John said, 'I am not afraid of being tried, or exiled, or even killed. All these things would be a glory to me, for it's only those who have proved themselves worthy that the Lord allows to suffer for his name. I am not afraid of anything except sin. If I am without guilt before the Lord, why should I care what anyone tries to do to me?'

'We are not afraid for you,' said Serapion, 'but for ourselves. What would the church in Constantinople be without you?'

'Don't talk like that,' John said sternly. 'The Church belongs to Christ, not to me. He will preserve it no matter what. He died for it – I didn't! So, don't be afraid, either for me or for yourselves.'

As they were still talking, there was a knock at the door. A moment later the servant came in, looking astonished. 'Archbishop,' he said, 'Two Libyan bishops are here to see you. They come as messengers from The Oak.'

'Let them in,' John said calmly, as his friends all stared at each other in horror.

The two men, with faces like stone, came in. They did not bow to the archbishop but wore sneers as they looked around the humble men there with distaste.

'We bring a letter from the Archbishop of Alexandria,' one of them said, and opened a scroll, which he began to read.

'John of Antioch:

We have received lists containing endless serious charges against you. Therefore, present yourself before us for trial.'

John stood slowly, quivering with anger. 'You bring this letter from a priest accused himself of crimes and ungodly behaviour, and acting outside his jurisdiction, without even the courtesy of naming the charges or addressing me as the archbishop?' He glanced behind him. 'Serapion, we will send a reply. Write for me, if you would.'

'Yes, John.' Serapion hurried to a desk and took out a quill and ink.

'Write this down. "I know it is true that Theophilus said both at Alexandria and in Lycia that, 'I am going to the capital to depose John,' and that is what he intends, for he has refused to meet or communicate with me ever since he set foot in Constantinople. If a man has acted thus against me before my trial, what would he not do after it? I now give you notice that you will not hear from me again, however often you write. The Archbishop of Constantinople.'"

Serapion dried the ink and handed the page to the Libyan bishops.

'You two,' John told them fiercely, 'should be ashamed of yourselves, taking part in this ridiculous charade of justice.'

One of the men looked down at the ground, but the other laughed. 'Save it for your trial, old man.'

Judgement

John went about his business. He continued to read new commentaries, write sermons condemning the selfishness of the rich, and encourage his congregation. But soon it was clear that the court, which so hated his criticism of their luxurious ways, had turned against him too. It was obvious that he had no one left in the palace on his side when a notary turned up with a summons from the emperor. He cleared his throat, opened his scroll and began to read.

Archbishop, you are aware that an ecclesiastical council has been convened against you across the Bosphorus, at one house called The Oak, in Chalcedon. You have refused to attend this council, which has received charges of the most serious nature against you, and now the emperor Arcadius demands your presence there along with your priests Serapion and Tigrius.

'You may return to the emperor the same reply which I gave to the summons from The Oak,' John returned. 'Many of those gathered there have stated themselves openly to be my enemies. There is no hope of a fair trial

107

while those men have charge of it, and I will not expose myself to this joke of a trial run by a rascal who himself still has unanswered charges against him. And by the way, is someone going to tell me eventually what I'm accused of?'

The notary bowed with stiff dignity and turned on his heels.

But it was not long before the list of accusations was made known – to everyone, for with the many angry enemies John had at The Oak, the gossip spread quickly all over Constantinople.

- John of Antioch sacked John the Deacon from his job for beating a slave, but beats slaves himself.
- John of Antioch has slandered and belittled his priests and put some in prison with no reason.
- John of Antioch has met women in suspicious circumstances.
- John of Antioch ate sweets in church after Communion.
- John of Antioch uses inappropriate terms in his sermons, including 'I was beside myself with joy.'
- John of Antioch eats in private so that he can indulge his secret overeating.
- John of Antioch does not practice hospitality.

'Remember that bishop, years ago, who said he would season your soup for you?' Serapion asked dryly. 'That last one has his mark on it, I reckon.'

'Well,' John said, striking his palm with his finger, 'these are all so patently ridiculous that I feel all the more that it would only hurt my dignity to answer them at all. What cheers me, though, is that the Lord's trial was so similar. He too had to answer for charges that were no true charges at all, and for a pack of lies devised by a throng of villains. I rejoice he has found me worthy to suffer so. I sent one of the deacons to tell them so, in response to their latest summons.'

'John, you don't seem to be suffering much at all in this trial. That's one of the most extraordinary things about it.'

'Well, as the great Paul said, *this* suffering truly isn't worthy to be compared to the glory that lies before us. This is nothing but the evil workings of a ridiculous man. Now, I know perfectly well that there may be serious consequences, but as I said before, I am not afraid of those.'

The two men were distracted by a strange noise, the clang of the door followed by an immensely heavy clatter coming closer and closer to them. John threw open the door to find his messenger standing there with huge chains heaped on him and tears in his eyes.

'A message from The Oak,' he said, holding out his arms. 'Theophilus says these will be on you before too long.'

John was stunned into silence for a second, but then he scoffed and set about unwinding the chains from the poor deacon. 'That stupid man. What do I care about chains? He really seems to think he could do something that would bother me. Something that could trouble my soul. The fool!'

But Theophilus didn't content himself with threats and summons for long. The next letter that arrived at the archbishop's palace was from the emperor. John looked at it, said 'Hmm,' and handed it to Serapion before heading upstairs.

John of Antioch:

You have refused to obey an imperial summons ordering you to attend the Synod of The Oak, where there are many accusations made against you. In answer to this disobedience, you are removed from the archbishopric of Constantinople and sentenced to exile.

Arcadius

'John!' Serapion called, hurrying after him. 'Wait! Where are you going – packing?'

John snorted. 'I have nothing I need to keep in this world. The Word of God lives in my mind, and while I would like to keep my friends' letters, those friends live in my heart. What else would I take – my fine clothes? My jewels and crowns? My golden spoons and ivory carvings?'

Serapion smiled: this was, as always, the John he knew. 'Then why do you hurry away from me?'

'Oh, I've got a sermon to write for Sunday, and inspiration struck. A change of subject.'

'But you can't preach! John, you can ignore the fools at The Oak all you want, but you can't ignore the fool in the palace. Unfair it may be, just as Christ's trial was unfair, but the sentence will be carried out all the same. You are leaving us. You think they'll let you into the church?'

'Am I leaving you? Perhaps I will leave the city, but I will not leave my people. Christ united me to his Church in this place – against my will, perhaps, but it was done, and it was as permanent as the union between husband and wife. No emperor of this world can remove me from it. If I cannot preach this sermon myself, then I will write it down, and one of my faithful friends will preach it for me. But no, I *will* preach once more.'

'And how do you propose to do that? I expect the imperial guard at the door any moment to carry you away.'

'Ha! Don't you know Constantinople? The people love me – and they are a people of a strong will. The emperor fears them. You think they will let me go without a fight? Arcadius will never dare to seize me on church grounds. Already the word spreads – look outside.'

Serapion joined John at the window. A huge throng of people was gathering outside the window, dozens running every minute to join them, deserting their shops, their sickbeds, their desks, to cling together outside the archbishop's palace. Women with babies in their arms and toddlers clinging to their skirts cried as loudly as their infants. Students and young men gathered across the square, outside the imperial palace, yelling out slogans and insults against the emperor.

'Theophilus was wise to move out to Chalcedon,' Serapion observed.

'Wise?' John replied dryly. 'No, only clever. He foresaw this a long time ago. But he has none of the wisdom of God. And I – perhaps I could have been clever too and played him at his game and won, but I preferred the wisdom of Christ who, "when accused, did not answer back". Those who truly know Christ will recognise that wisdom.'

'This will spill into riots and bloodshed.'

'Look at them,' John murmured. 'These poor ones, who never before had a bishop who really loved their souls above the things of this world. These dear ones. I never thought I would come to love them so.' He sighed and looked at Serapion. 'Don't worry. I'll preach against any violence in my name. I'll preach in favour of my own sentence, if I must. And if the city still threatens violence, and the emperor does not relent, I'll give myself up.'

'Can I say something?'

'Always.'

'John, it's – it's been a very great honour. You know, having you here, working so closely …'

John smiled and grasped Serapion's shoulder. 'My friend, don't say goodbye just yet.'

The Last Sermon

People were continually drawn to the Archbishop's palace over Saturday night, and nobody seemed to leave. The noise of the people's shouts and cries was so loud that John couldn't sleep a wink. He pictured Arcadius and Eudokia in their golden rooms, pacing in front of the bed, their children wailing with exhaustion, all wondering what the furious people of the city were going to do. Would the threat be enough to make the emperor back down and reverse his sentence?

Oh Lord, wherever I go, you walk with me, John prayed. *I confess exile is not my choice, but I choose whatever path you lay before me. Thank you for counting me worthy to suffer so like Christ. Help me to conduct myself worthy of that honour.*

As dawn broke John looked out the window. The whole of the city, from his palace down to the harbour, from the tip of the Acropolis to the far end of the Hippodrome, was one solid sea of people, every face turned toward his door.

John tied on his cloak and slipped on his battered shoes, wondering how far they would have to take him.

His servants and deacons, some of whom had stayed over at the palace, were slowly creaking to life.

'John?' Serapion asked, rubbing his eyes as he met John in the hall.

'Up so late, on so momentous a day?' John asked, smiling. 'It's time we left for the cathedral. So much to do on a Sunday morning before the service can begin.'

Serapion threw up his hands. 'A noble effort to try, but the soldiers will arrest you the moment you set foot on your own doorstep!'

'Have faith, brother. We have to do nothing but part the waters.'

'Archbishop?'

'Come, follow close behind me.'

John took a breath and opened the door. The crowds fell silent. 'A good Lord's day to you all,' John said in his usual brisk voice, and then, turning toward the guards who waited with their chains, 'And to you, officers.'

'John of Antioch,' said the captain, 'you have been convicted of –'

No one heard another word he said, for the crowd immediately erupted into a fury. 'You won't set a hand on our archbishop! We have more swords than you do, you cowards! Draw a weapon on him and we'll storm the palace!'

The guards hesitated. John held his hand up for quiet. 'This is not the time, or you'll cause a deadly riot,' he said to the captain, so quietly that no one else could hear him. 'If the emperor does not turn, I'll surrender to you in a safer place.'

The guard nodded and stepped back, though he continued to eye up the crowd menacingly.

'Come, Archbishop,' said a large man standing among the crowd. 'We will guard you on your way to Hagia Sophia.'

'Shed no blood in my name, son,' said John. 'These guards will not trouble me for now.'

The crowds parted, clearing John's way to the cathedral door, watching suspiciously for any sign of charging soldiers. But the captain was as good as his word, and John reached Hagia Sophia without harm, though his walk had taken somewhat longer than usual as he stopped to comfort or lay his hand on some of the people. The church itself felt huge inside, so empty after the bustle and shoving of the square. Its cool silence was soothing. As John made his way to his study, to reflect again on his sermon, it occurred to him that now he was the one finding sanctuary in this building. Yet he would not cling to the altar but preside over it.

As he had known it would be, the church was packed by the time he came out to preach, the air stifling between the oil lamps and the incense and the hundreds of people. And for once, he didn't have to shush their chattering and gossiping when he started to address them. Every tongue was silent, every eye on him, their tears glittering in the lamplight.

'My dear flock,' he said, 'You are all so afraid for me. And I am grateful to you for loving me so much, but don't you realise there's no reason? What should I fear – death? "For to me to live is Christ, and to die is gain."[1] Exile? "The earth is the LORD'S and the fullness thereof."[2] Loss of property? "We brought nothing into the world and we cannot take anything out of the world."[3]'

'And don't think these things are so terrible that the world has never seen such crimes before. I have more than enough examples for the suffering I am to go through. If the empress wants to have me sawn in two, I have Isaiah for a pattern. If she wants to throw me into the sea, I shall remember Jonah. Throw me into a furnace? There Shadrach, Meschach and Abednego walked with our Lord. Cut off my head? That was the privilege of John the Baptist, whom Christ called "the greatest of the prophets". There is nothing that the followers of Jesus have not endured long before our time, and nothing, *nothing* has been found that could separate them from his love and care.'

After the service, the people ensured that John was delivered back to his house in safety, lining the way so that the soldiers were kept at a distance, glaring both at people and priests. But the whole city still felt the threat of losing their beloved preacher, and the people were

---

1. Philippians 1:21.

2. Psalm 24:1.

3. 1 Timothy 6:7.

restless, muttering dark things against the emperor and empress, not to mention Theophilus and his gang still cowering up at The Oak.

The next morning John decided to go back up to Hagia Sophia to minister to both his people and his deacons and priests. It seemed the right place to be; hiding away in his house made him restless and grumpy. Besides, he might not have much time. He needed to be with his people every minute he could. Once again the people guarded him on his way to the cathedral. But he had not been there long when the deaconess, Olympias, came up to him.

'Archbishop,' she said in a trembling voice, 'they're really going to do it. The guard is going to take you by force when you leave here today, people or no people. The empress has had enough of this waiting.'

'If they take me in full view of the people, there will be bloodshed,' John murmured. 'I would rather they be free of that guilt, even if the guards bring it on themselves. Didn't even the Jewish judges understand that they must take Jesus in Gethsemane, far away from where they might cause a riot?' He drove his finger into his palm. 'Well, if they're not wise enough to take that route, we are. I want you to tell the guards to meet me at the side entrance. The people won't be expecting that.'

Olympias hurried away, and John spent a few minutes in prayer. He heard a cheer as the soldiers marched away; the people must have thought they'd given up. They had no idea the soldiers were coming at John's own request to take him away.

John walked quietly to the side door. On the way he passed Serapion. 'Goodbye,' John said cheerfully, but grabbed his friend's arm. 'Pray for me.'

Serapion stared at him, and then a light of understanding dawned in his face. *Goodbye* meant goodbye for good. 'And you for me,' he said quietly.

John walked on, opened the side door to let in a shaft of light, and stepped out into the hard Constantinople sun. It glinted off the soldiers' blades, nearly blinding him. 'Well, officers,' he said, 'we'd better be quick before there's a disturbance.'

One of the soldiers approached him with a chain.

'Do you really think you need that, son?' John asked with a raised eyebrow. 'Besides, if the people see me chained, they will be all the angrier. I suggest we just go quickly.'

The officer nodded. Two of them grabbed John's arms and they started to march down to the imperial harbour of Bucoleon.

Of course they could not get far, marching through Constantinople's main square with their prey, before people noticed. The little group attracted a growing, wailing collection of followers until, by the time they arrived at the harbour, it felt like the whole desperate mob that had gathered outside Hagia Sophia was now milling and shouting at the harbour instead.

The soldiers, stony-faced, shoved John onto a small ship. 'You are free to go where you want, so long as you never return to Constantinople,' said an officer. 'The captain is at your service.'

John nodded and turned to the ship's captain. 'Can you wait a moment? I want to commend the people to God.'

He nodded, and John turned to face the shore, raising his hands and his voice.

'Dear ones, see that you do no violence in my name. Christ forgave his enemies and you can be sure I do the same. So, you must forgive them as well. It may be that a church council can still be convened to overturn this ridiculous sentence, for you know that I am innocent of all the accusations I've faced. But for now, I ask only that you pray for me, as I do for you. And remember to give thanks. Job suffered worse than I have, and what did he say? *The Lord gave, and the Lord has taken away; blessed be the name of the Lord.*'[4]

He turned away. 'You may set sail for the Hieron, sir – I won't trouble you to go far. I have a friend to visit near Nicomedia, and there I may wait to see if there can be any justice for me in this city.'

4. Job 1:21.

The City without John

John had requested his followers not to shed any blood
on his behalf, but they loved him so much that his loss
drove them into a sort of frenzy. They massed around
the churches and the palace walls, crazy with anger,
demanding their archbishop back. Theophilus chose
this moment, his victory over John, to sail majestically
across the channel and preside over the church in John's
place. The people were outraged at his behaviour.

'Did you hear that he brought back and honoured
some of the corrupt priests that John had fired?' one
screamed to another.

'Not only that, one of his sidekicks had the nerve
to preach against John! For his pride! In one of *his own
churches!*'

'This Egyptian is riding through the streets waving
and smiling, as if he'd delivered us from some enemy,
not stolen our beloved father away from us!'

'Theophilus must pay!'

'The emperor must pay!'

'To the palace!'

The emperor, trembling behind his thick walls, called out the imperial troops to drive the people back into their place. Monks were killed along with some of the common people who were protesting. But the people didn't go home – they were too angry. The only one who went home was Theophilus, retreating back to The Oak in fear of his life.

The emperor had faced the people's displeasure before. It was not such an unusual thing for the city to be in uproar for one reason or another; all great cities have passionate people who take to the streets, who hate the government, who campaign for changes. Constantinople was no different.

But this time, it seemed that God was on the people's side.

'It was the wrong move forcing him out,' Arcadius frowned to his wife. 'But after all, you were the one who wanted him out of sight. The one thing you and Eutropius agreed on.'

'Me?' asked the empress, shaking with fear even as the walls thrummed with the noise of the people's chants. 'I never wanted this! How can you say such a thing?'

'But Eudokia! You hated John – you've been looking for a reason to have him punished!'

'That wasn't *me*,' Eudokia shouted. 'That was my friends he insulted, wasn't it! Going up to The Oak and supporting that hideous Egyptian archbishop.'

'But you supported them doing it! You sent them to come and report back!'

'Well, I didn't know how it was going to turn out! Who knew the common people loved him so – none of the people *we* know did!'

Suddenly there was a mighty shout from outside, just as the palace walls began to shake and crumble. Eudokia screamed and fell to her face in front of her husband. 'An earthquake! God's judgement is on us! Please, Arcadius, send and bring him back. You must bring him back! Or – or –'

She gasped, clutching her pregnant belly, and then fainted away.

'You!' Arcadius shouted, pointing at a servant. 'Call for the empress's physician. And get Briso the chamberlain here. He's to take a message to John of Antioch, no matter where he is by now. Find the captain of the ship that took him away. Find out where he's gone.'

Within hours, Briso was on a ship, having taken down a tearful, panicked letter from the suffering empress. The city's people, from whom nothing was ever kept secret for long, were there as always – half cheering his departure, half threatening lest he should come back without their preacher.

A few hours' sail took Briso to the Hieron, and it was not difficult to find out where John was staying, given that the whole region talked about nothing else. Briso was one of John's few friends at court, so he was not nervous about talking to the archbishop, but he was wondering how to persuade a man who had been so outrageously insulted to return to the site of his injustice.

John came to meet Briso as soon as he was announced. 'Come and sit,' he said cheerfully, as if nothing had happened. 'Some water? An apple?'

Briso smiled at John's offer, as simple as ever despite staying in a fashionable house that could offer wine and honey cakes. Any house in this region would have been overwhelmed with the honour of having both an archbishop and a high-ranking government official at the same time, but then, if the host was a friend of John's, he was probably less than impressed with such worldly matters.

'I hope you are well despite the inconvenience of your journey,' Briso said.

John smiled with a raised eyebrow. 'My friend, speak plainly. You hope I am well despite my *exile*. And I assure you I am. But what is your message? Am I to be moved to a place further away, a place I did *not* choose?'

'Not exactly. Sir, may I read you a letter from the empress?'

'Certainly.'

John sat down on a couch and waited expectantly.

'To the Archbishop John.

Your Holiness must not suppose that I had anything to do with your trial or sentence. I am innocent of this whole matter. This conspiracy is the work of corrupt and wicked men, but I am grief-stricken, remembering that my children were baptised by you. God, whom I serve, is witness of my tears. The city is in disarray, your spiritual children left bereft and mourning, as I am myself. We beg you to return and have sent our fastest ship to convey you home.'

'A very interesting epistle,' John said, nodding. 'So she had nothing to do with it? That's a surprise. She did not exactly bid me goodbye with tears running down her face. Or at all, for that matter.'

'Sir, what can I say?' Briso asked, wincing with shame. 'You know the empress.'

'Indeed, I do. What has transpired in the last three days to bring about this change of heart? Riots? Surely that was expected.'

'The riots, yes. The earthquake was less expected.'

'Earthquake? I've heard nothing about an earthquake.'

'So the empress says. Some others in the palace felt it, but not all. She was hysterical with fear. There is talk that she has lost the child she was carrying because of it. A judgement on the city, she says. No one is quite sure what happened.'

'Her conscience is tormenting her superstitious heart,' John said. 'And the emperor, does he add his plea to hers? Does he take back his sentence?'

'You'll find his invitation here, but it's rather less emotional.' Briso presented a document with the imperial seal. John took it and read it silently. It was a matter-of-fact, official document ending his exile.

'Archbishop,' Briso finally said, 'we have no right to summon you back to the city after all the injustice you've suffered. The court with all its hypocrisy, its coddling of Theophilus and his lies, they have done you a great wrong. A man of even ordinary pride would never consider –'

John tutted him into silence. 'Hush, man, talking of injustice and pride. Is my life my own, or does it belong to Christ? And if he calls me back to my people, is that not evidence of his goodness and faithfulness to me? Justice will be restored. And while the empress is somewhat deceptive in her claims that she never conspired against me, I shall pray that this panicked plea turns to real repentance. I am, as she points out so forcefully, her pastor too.'

'Then you'll return? At once?'

'Of course, good and faithful servant. You did not doubt me, I hope.'

Briso sighed in relief. 'I don't place my confidence in men acting honourably, Archbishop. I've been part of the court far too long for that.'

John laughed. 'God will do his work even in the court, don't fear. Now, I understand there is a ship waiting for us?'

Back to the City

The first time he had sailed to Constantinople, John hadn't been much interested in the skyline of the great city. But now, returning home, he found it a truly glorious sight. The whole capital had heard of his return, and under the glimmer of moonlight, the dark water of the Bosphorus was alive with boats magnificently lit and decorated in his honour. The great chain that stretched from the imperial shore to the Pera shore had been opened, and as he sailed into the Golden Horn there was a sweet distant music as the people lined the sea walls, singing hymns and waving torches. Never had the city looked so beautiful.

'The riots that met your departure have been replaced by even greater beauty and peace,' Briso murmured. 'Perhaps this is what it's like to arrive in heaven.'

'The sea has become a city and the city one huge church,' John laughed. 'A beautiful sight indeed.' He raised a hand in blessing as they passed one of the decorated boats, its sailors shouting out to him happily.

'Chalcedon looks rather dark and deserted by comparison,' Briso pointed out, gazing across the water to the suburb.

'What has become of Theophilus?'

'He tried to enter your churches with his henchmen. The city threatened to attack him and he had to retreat back to The Oak.'

'But he is still near,' John said, turning to Briso. 'My friend, I must not enter the city walls – not yet.'

'But all these people waiting for you!'

'Yes, but I am still under condemnation by a church court. If I take my position again with that verdict still standing, it will give opportunity for my enemies to slander me again. They will say I'm defying justice. Arcadius has invited me back, but he has not condemned their corrupt council.'

'What are we to do then?' Briso asked, flinging out his arms.

'I suggest we turn aside to Pera – there must be some house there that will take me in. It's still part of the city, but it keeps a distance from my home and church so that it's clear I have not re-entered the cathedral in defiance of any judgement against me.'

'The empress owns a house in Pera,' Briso said. 'I daresay she'll be glad to take credit for lending it to you – even if she didn't know it was her idea.'

'I'll accept her hospitality,' John laughed. 'You must order the captain to change course, quickly, before we come too near to the royal harbour.'

Briso saw John to the empress's house, where her startled servants had to try hard to restrain their joy at the sight of him. John greeted them warmly, then looked round the elegant parlour and sighed. 'Will I never get used to all this gold and mosaic and coloured drapes and embroidered pillows?'

Briso laughed. 'I trust you will be with us long enough that even you will get used to them one day. I must sail for the harbour, Archbishop, and tell the emperor where you are, and why. I'm sure some of your priests and deacons will want to come to you, too, if you can't go to them.'

'I'd welcome their company very much. We have a great deal to discuss.'

John waved Briso off and then took a moment to stand on the porch outside, looking across the Golden Horn, the columns and rooftop of his own church mighty and huge against the night sky. He took comfort from the nearness of it, and the surety that it would remain long after his death.

He could still see the torches burning bright along the shore, but they seemed to waver wildly as if the people were now searching for him up and down the walls. There was no longer a sweet hum of song, but now an angry buzz of voices as they wondered where their archbishop had gone. Briso was returning to a people disappointed – and that was always a dangerous people in Constantinople. Surely the emperor would overturn the finding of The Oak quickly, before the city erupted again.

It was still morning when a ship arrived from the city, with thirty of John's priests on board. They flooded into the palace where he was waiting to greet them, crowded round him and pressed his hands and arms, laughing with surprised joy to see him again so soon. Serapion couldn't stop grinning as they all sat down.

'But what are we doing here, in the empress's summer house?' one of them cried. 'We should all be round the familiar table in the archbishop's palace. The whole city was a party last night, John, ready for your arrival, and now there are grumblings again.'

'It's thought that Theophilus is behind your delay,' another added. 'The mob talks of going out to The Oak and throwing him into the sea.'

'Theophilus has nothing to do with it – directly, at least,' John said. 'I can't go back to my home and church until I'm declared innocent by a church council, preferably one that isn't stacked against me. The emperor must act quickly, all the more so if the people are angry.'

He didn't have long to wait. As they sat there talking, the State Minister arrived on the emperor's beautiful little ship, *Greyhound*. He walked up to John and bent low as the other priests glanced at each other, smiling over his head.

'Honoured Archbishop,' he breathed, still bowed.

'Am I?' John asked. 'I understand I've been deposed.'

'The emperor recognises the injustice done by the Council of The Oak, and begs his spiritual father to re-enter the city, which thirsts for the blessing of God to return upon it, and to ascend the patriarchal throne without delay.'

John gave a cough, trying not to laugh at this flowery court language. 'Well, one always likes to be invited, but the emperor hasn't the authority simply to pardon in church matters. He must convene a new church council to overturn the decision, or I shall have no authority in the city, and The Oak may persecute me again with fresh grounds.'

'The emperor will do as you ask, Your Holiness. But to convene a council takes time, and the city is in great distress and violent roiling over the absence of its loving shepherd, without whom it is as a lost –'

'I get the point,' John said dryly. 'They're about to riot again and no one else can calm them. I suppose we had better take ship, then.'

'Thank you, O blessed one. Truly you are as gracious as you are …'

'Late?' John suggested. 'Come along, brothers, I should think the emperor's ship will be big enough to carry us all over the Horn.'

It was clear even from the Pera shore that the opposite bank was crowded with people all along the sea walls. The noise was still a distant grumble as the *Greyhound* set sail, but by the time it had rounded the point of the city, coming into view of the palace, there was near silence as the people craned their eyes to see whether John was on board. As they neared the Bucoleon harbour, the sea walls erupted into cheers that put the crowd even at the most exciting Hippodrome tournament to shame. As John stepped onto the shore of the royal harbour the noise was so great that he could not hear either his own priests' exclamations of joy or the State Minister's many fancy words. The imperial guard, who had arrested him three or four days earlier, now stood by as a guard of honour. And when John emerged from the harbour walls into the public street at the back of the palace, the people danced and wept with joy, breaking out into psalms and falling to their knees with gratitude.

The people moved like a sea, the tide carrying John irresistibly all down the length of the Hippodrome to Hagia Sophia, which itself was already full to bursting of those who had run ahead to carry him into the great stone-carved pulpit. John raised his hands for silence, but still he had to shout over the excitement of the congregation.

'What shall I say? What shall I say? Blessed be God! That is what I said when I went away, and that is what I say now, and that is what I say all the time. You remember that I quoted Job and said, "Blessed be the name of the LORD."[1] That was the blessing I left with you, and that is the thanksgiving I repeat now. I gave thanks when I was exiled, and I give thanks when I come back.

'I say these things to encourage you to bless God at all times. If good things happen, bless God! If bad

---

1. Job 1:21.

things happen, still bless God, and the bad has no power to hurt you.

'The games are on today, and no one is there! You have all poured into church like a river, and your voices stream up to heaven in praises of love to the Father. There are plenty of sheep today, but no sign of a wolf. They have all run away. Who has driven them off? Not I, the shepherd, but you, the noble sheep!'

John finally made it back to his own home, his own table with its simple food rather than the rich offerings his hosts had tried to press on him, his own humble, loving servants who grasped his hands with wordless delight, and his own bed.

When he arrived at his palace, there was another letter waiting for him from the empress.

Dear John, our blessed father,

My prayers have been fulfilled and my greatest goals completed. I have earned a crown better than that of the imperial throne itself. I have brought back the high priest; I have restored the head to the body, the pilot to the ship, the shepherd to the flock —

'That's probably enough,' John said, stopping Serapion's gleeful reading. 'I'm happy she's happy.'

Serapion laughed. 'Well, it's good to know a ruler can be humble enough to change her mind.'

'Yes, but only repentance changes the heart. Let's hope she's humble enough for that. If she were honest she would send apologies, not congratulate herself on a job well done. Not that I am looking for an apology, but I wish for her own sake to see her change her heart and not just her tune.'

'Whatever has brought this change about, I welcome it,' Serapion returned. 'Like our Lord at his death, you were only called away from your people for three days. But the storm had been building for such a long time, and the victory seems the greater for it.'

'The people rejoiced more than I would have wished,' John replied. 'I would much rather that they were so overjoyed on Easter, celebrating Christ's victory over death, or indeed every Sunday when they can come to church and worship the Risen One. Instead they flood the streets to dance and sing over this temporary triumph.'

'Temporary?'

John smiled wearily. 'Serapion, don't forget that every triumph belonging to this world is temporary. We haven't seen the last of storms.'

A New Storm

John was used to the distracting noise from the Hippodrome crowds while trying to carry on his Sunday service, but this – this was unbelievable. Here he was, trying to prepare his people for Communion, and he could barely even hear himself preach. The congregation, smaller than usual, craned their necks restlessly toward the thunderous din just outside the cathedral. There were even fewer pickpockets than usual – they were targeting the much bigger crowds in the public square. After two months, the magic of John's triumphant return was old news. There was a more exciting show in town, and as was often the case, it was the extravagant, glamorous empress.

'I see that you are distracted today,' John reprimanded the congregation. 'Remember what Jesus said of John the Baptist. "What did you go out to see? A man dressed in fine clothes? No, those who wear fine clothes are in kings' palaces. Then what did you go out to see? A prophet? Yes, I tell you, and more than a prophet (NIV)[1]"

---

1. Matthew 11:8-9.

'You, Constantinople, you came to see a preacher – but you are not even listening to him. In your minds you are picturing what is happening outside the palace, with those men in rich clothes. Is not the Augusteion a public square? May you not leave right now, and see with your own eyes what is happening, that you're so curious about? You all know very well what it is.

'The empress is raising a monument to herself. A pedestal proclaiming in Latin and Greek her own greatness, topped by a pillar of purple marble, then a silver statue of herself. I do not doubt that the statue, like the lady herself, is beautiful. Is it, do you think, more beautiful than the Body and Blood of the Lord that you see laid out before you for Communion?'

'"But," you are thinking, "tomorrow all the city will be discussing the ceremonies that are going on right now. They will be talking about the extravagant games, the songs and entertainment, the sweetmeats and wine that are flowing in the square, the blushing empress and proud emperor as they see her honoured. And we know nothing about it."'

'Well, you are free to leave if you wish. You may as well go, if you are not going to listen to a word of the sermon or pay complete attention to the Lord's Supper. Certainly, I am not John the Baptist, due a prophet's honour. But I caution you to take care in attending instead the worldly court of Herodias.'

The people, startled into silence, blushed to a man and turned to face the front as John continued his planned sermon.

But John was wrong – the talk of the town the next day wasn't Eudokia's statue. It was his sermon. It wasn't long before the city prefect showed up at the Archbishop's palace to discuss it.

'I have heard a great deal about your sermon,' he said, grim-faced. '"Again Herodias storms and runs wild, again she dances, again she asks for John's head on a platter." Oh, and referring to the priests of the palace chapels as "priests of Baal" – a little dramatic, don't you think.'

'I said neither of those things,' John said calmly. 'You have heard greatly exaggerated reports. I cautioned the people against paying greater attention to the things of the court than the things of God. If anyone has cause to complain, it is I, that such an unruly and disruptive court ceremony should be held outside the very walls of the cathedral during a service. It was nothing but a challenge from the court.'

'Come, Archbishop. We know very well that you are no friend of the empress. She feels the insult of your words as keenly as a knife in her breast.'

'She feels an imagined insult, since I never used those words. And you are wrong – no one cares more for the empress's soul than I. I baptised her children, I have given her wise and loving counsel; I even returned to the city at her request despite my grave mistreatment.'

'You returned due to her gracious forgiveness, despite being deposed by a council of your own church.'

'Come now! You know very well that has been condemned as an unlawful trial by sixty bishops here in Constantinople.'

'Ah, but they never met in a formal council,' said the prefect with a sneer, as he turned to go. 'But don't worry, we'll fix that. The empress has already sent letters to several most dignified bishops, summoning them to a *new* council. The matter will soon be settled once and for all.'

After the prefect left, John spent some time in silent prayer. Then he sent for Serapion, Olympias, and some other close friends, and told them of the prefect's words.

'His meaning is clear,' Serapion said. 'The empress has sent again for Theophilus. They say when he got back to Alexandria, his people met him with boos and jeering due to his dishonourable conduct here. No doubt he will be glad to return to the capital where at least he has his supporters.'

'The common people here will be furious if he returns,' John replied. 'He had to sneak away by night just to get away safely. When the people realise there is a new threat against me…'

'But the empress is determined, if she is personally writing to your enemies,' Serapion argued. 'The people can be persuasive, but the empress has the power.'

'It's the emperor who has the power,' another argued. 'We must appeal to him.'

'But the empress has power over the emperor.'

'Their power is not absolute,' said Olympias quietly. 'What is the power of this world if it's God who decides John's fate?'

'Well said,' John told her. 'We will not be afraid, dear ones. I had hoped this trial would not resume so soon, but God will hold us fast, even if in exile or death. I know the empress will not accept an incomplete victory this time. If she determines I am to go, then I will not expect so easy a return. I did not mean to compare her to Herodias so starkly as she thinks, but it may well be that she will demand my head on a platter.'

He saw his friends shiver at the thought.

'I'm not saying all this to worry you,' he told them. 'Rather, you must prepare yourselves to encourage and build up the church without me. No preacher stays with his church forever, and you are to carry on my work. What does it matter if I'm not with you, if you still have the Holy Spirit? Who would you rather have?'

'We'd rather have both,' Serapion said with a weak smile.

'But I would gladly lay down my life if it meant you would all be greatly filled with the Spirit,' John told him. 'As I trust you will be. I sense that the church here is called to a time of suffering, dark as a night with no moon. But that is not to be our concern yet. While it is still day, we work.'

Eudokia's letters worked with amazing speed. Within weeks, bishops and priests were again flooding into the city – from regions that had no authority whatsoever in the Constantinople church, including representatives from Theophilus, who didn't dare show his face in the city again. But that didn't matter. They were there by imperial decree, and even though the emperor should have no power in the church, John was not willing to forge an open conflict between the church and the court. Nor did the opposing bishops meet in a formal council – the disaster of The Oak had already shown that that would provoke outrage from the people – but both sides met in huge, informal, noisy gatherings that argued endlessly and settled nothing.

'This so-called archbishop returned to his church without authority! He had been deposed – he is no true priest at all!'

'Deposed against the law, by a supposed "council" that had no right to meet in this city, composed of outsiders and enemies.'

'They *had* to meet to convict him of his terrible crimes!'

'Of which he wasn't even convicted. All they could prove is that he didn't go before the council when the emperor summoned him.'

'A crime in itself! What more have we to prove? He disobeyed the emperor, the Equal of the Apostles!'[2]

---

2. This was one of the titles used by the Byzantine emperors – despite the fact that most were highly corrupt and immoral.

'An unlawful summons to an unlawful council.'

'That's not how the emperor sees it.'

'Anyway, John was restored by a greater assembly of sixty bishops – ones that actually had a right to meet in Constantinople.'

'But never in a formal council, which means The Oak still stands.'

On and on it went. But the seriousness of the situation was obvious just a few weeks later, when the emperor refused to come to Hagia Sophia for the Christmas service. How could he sit under the leadership of an archbishop with open charges unanswered against him? John went ahead and preached as usual on the wonders of God come down to man.

More months went by. John presided over Lent, counselling his people to fast and pray as they prepared for the great Communion season to come. It was a sober time as they worried that this would be John's last Easter among them. A great many prepared to be baptised, knowing this would be their last chance to have John do this for them.

Days before Easter, a message arrived from the palace – delivered by the imperial guards.

As a formally deposed bishop, it is not lawful for John of Antioch to preside over the celebration of Easter at the Great Church. For his own protection he is now placed under house arrest to await the decision of a church council.

Arcadius

John did not have to think before returning his message to the emperor. 'If a lawful church council is actually convened, I will be more than happy to go and appear before it. But I have received this church from God, and I am responsible for the spiritual wellbeing of my flock. I am not free to desert my duties, and so I shall carry on. The city is yours and you can turn me out by force if you wish. And on your head be it.'

The city was set for a battle.

War Against the Church

The cathedral was full of lamplight, the scent of incense, and the sweet murmur of the church singers practicing their hymns. The great marble cover had been removed from the pool of water at the front of the church, and hundreds of women were in the smaller chapels, changing into pure white baptismal gowns. It was the custom for new Christians to be baptised on Easter Eve, so that they could take Communion for the first time on the great holiday of Christ's resurrection. John, overseeing the priests' preparation of the wine and bread behind the altar, was filled with peace and contentment on this sweetest of occasions.

Then he heard the screams.

John and his priests stared up at each other, startled, and ran out into the main church. Dozens of soldiers were streaming through the great doors, weapons drawn, slashing with their swords, roughly shoving worshippers with their heavy shields. The people ran in terror, trying to hide or make their way to the side doors, priests guiding them as best they could in the chaos. The screams were coming from the chapels, the women converts running out half-dressed and covered with blood, chased by the soldiers.

'How dare you!' John shouted, running at one of the men.

'This is an unlawful service run by a deposed bishop!' the man returned and knocked John down onto the blood-slicked floor. In a daze, John could see several of the men running toward the altar, and he scrambled to his feet to defend the most precious part of his church – but by the time he got there the Communion wine was knocked over, spattering the soldiers' clothes, mingling with the blood in the baptismal waters.

'Come on!' Olympias shouted, grabbing John's arm.

'I must stay and defend –'

'There is nothing to defend. The church is lost. You must gather the people elsewhere. That is the best thing you can do for them.'

He nodded, and they ran together, slipping across the wet marble to the door. Outside, the people trembled in the dark, crying and hiding in the shadows. 'We go to the Baths, where we may still baptise,' John shouted. 'God does not need the walls of a church to meet with us!'

And the people, terrified and shaken as they were, marched behind John. This persecution, this night, was not over – but they would not be stopped from celebrating the Resurrection with their beloved bishop. Hundreds trooped into the Baths, quiet and cool at this time of night, the men and fully dressed women helping to cover up the modesty of the half-dressed converts and bandage their wounds. But they had barely filed into the building, with one of the priests just beginning their opening prayers, when a military captain marched in and interrupted. 'John of Antioch, you will lead these people outside to disperse to their homes,' he commanded. 'You have no authority in the Church of this city.'

'I have the authority of Christ and of his people – the true Church,' John returned. 'Of which it seems you are not one. So, I must ask you to leave.'

The captain sneered and looked round the silent people. 'Go home and there will be no further violence. You can do nothing now for your former archbishop. Any baptism or Communion you receive from him will not be recognised by the Church in Constantinople. Beware lest you all receive the reward of heretics.'

In response, the people gathered closely around John, staring the captain down until he gave a curt nod and turned to go.

'This is a scandal,' the people whispered to each other tearfully. 'We were doing nothing but worshipping peacefully in our own church. What will they do next? To us? To John?'

'Children,' John said, above their murmur, 'we are not here to worry about our own future, which we know is safe in Christ. Instead we are to bring glory to God for Jesus' victory over death. And your presence here, in the face of such violence, *does* bring him glory, for it says that you love him more than you love your own lives.'

The rhythm of the soldiers' boots beat out an ominous tattoo on the marble floors. 'Go!' John said. 'Let there be no more bloodshed. We meet in the fields outside the city walls. Go quickly and I will meet you there, in the waste ground at Pempton. Bring all the faithful Christians you can find.'

The soldiers were upon them. The gleaming walls echoed with screams and the baths curdled with blood as the people again ran from the flashing swords.

But at dawn, the fields outside the city walls were crowded with people. There the people sang their psalms and hymns. There John preached on Christ's victory over death. And there, as soon as the emperor had been informed that hundreds of 'heretics' were worshipping outside the city, the soldiers attacked them one more time. That Easter morning, the true believers who followed John's teachings to love Christ rather than the world were killed and wounded and chased back to their homes. And at the same time, the superficial and fearful and ambitious people of the city were herded into services by the anti-John priests, with the help of the army, so that no one could say all the churches were empty on Easter morning. As for John, he was marched back to his palace like a naughty boy, and there he spent the rest of his Easter.

Although there was an imperial guard placed to watch John's door, his followers organised a guard of their own to defend him against attack or arrest, especially going back and forth from the palace to the church. One evening a slave, wrapped in a cloak, was lingering outside the archbishop's palace. Neither the soldiers nor the people's guard found this unusual, as many people, usually the poor, often came to stand outside the palace to pay their respects to the archbishop, perhaps in the hope of seeing him at a window. This man stood there for a while, drawing closer and closer – then, all of a sudden, he drew a long knife and rushed forward, slashing at both the official and unofficial guards near the door. One was killed but the others managed to hold the attacker down, getting cut as they wrestled the knife away. 'A priest paid me to kill John!' the slave cried. 'I had no choice – it was the priest!'

It could have been a priest who had paid the man to try and kill John, but people whispered about whether it was really the court. John's death would have made things a lot easier for them.

The spring ripened into a hot, humid summer. Constantinople enjoyed its cooling fruit drinks, its patio banquets with servants stirring up a breeze with their large feather fans, its pleasure boat cruises to the Princes Isles in the Bosphorus, cats lying languidly at the side of the road or taking refuge in the shade of church courtyards, the smell of the sea resting over the city, children dancing in the fountains.

The heat seemed to make John's enemies more restless, more impatient. There was an increase of rumours. The empress was on the warpath: she was getting heavy with yet another new baby, and the heat made her irritable. And so, the news came while John was in Hagia Sophia: he was no longer under house arrest. Instead he was going back into exile. The emperor had finally signed the order, and this time he was firm. Thoroughly sick of the whole business, with his palace priests and his wife nagging at him all the time, he wanted an immediate arrest and a destination from which John would not have so easy a return.

John took this news with a sigh. 'I am glad for my own sake, to have all this over with,' he said, 'but sorry for the grief it will give to the people.'

He called Serapion and Olympias and all his other dear ones into the baptistery, the more private space at the side of the cathedral. Closing the door, he said to them, 'The emperor has ordered my exile. I have finished my race, and I don't imagine you will see me again. So, listen carefully to my last words. Keep on with your kindness and generosity to the church, and if the next archbishop is elected fairly, give him your support. God will give you the grace.' He gazed all around their beloved faces, and for once it seemed that his breath caught in his throat, and tears filled his eyes. 'And pray for me.'

Olympias and the other deaconesses surrounded him, pressing his arms, kissing his hands and wetting them with their tears. 'Lead them out to the back,' John said quietly to Serapion. 'This sobbing will attract attention. The people mustn't know, or there will be riots. And have my riding mule brought to the main entrance, but do not open the doors yet.'

Serapion nodded. John took a long look at him as he gently guided the women to the back of the church. He went back to the church office to collect some of his papers and letters and stayed there for a moment, looking around that beloved little room, blinking hard to keep the tears at bay. He had not felt like this since – when? Leaving Antioch, probably, after his mother's death. Even now it was strange to think he would never see his hometown again. The emperor would certainly never allow him to take refuge in a place where he had so many supporters.

He left his office and glanced across the beautiful sanctuary to the main entrance. Serapion was waiting there to say goodbye, perhaps to go with him. John stood still. He and his friend looked at one another. Then John gave a slow nod and turned away. While his supporters outside the cathedral would be preparing to guard him and his mule, wondering where he could be going, ready to fight for him if necessary, John slipped out the side entrance and offered his hands for the guards' chains.

Letters in Exile

Dear John, Archbishop of Constantinople,

You left us quietly to spare the city violence, but I'm sure you knew that many of the people would not honour that intention. Of course, we all expected the rioting, and the persecution of those who remain faithful to you, but no one expected the ruin of the city. The night you left, in all the disorder, Hagia Sophia went on fire. The wooden roof blazed so fiercely that the fire soon leapt not only to nearby houses but even to the Senate and the palace. The Senate is destroyed, the palace greatly damaged, and our church, John, the beautiful Hagia Sophia, is left without one stone on top of another.

Your friends and followers refuse to worship with your enemies or the followers of the new archbishop, who in turn has no sympathy for your friends. The court has been persecuting us mercilessly, arresting and exiling some, torturing others even to death, accusing us of starting the fire ourselves — though none have offered any evidence or reason why we should destroy our beloved bishop's cathedral. Indeed, I have been accused of starting the fire with my own hands, but I simply laugh at such a ridiculous idea.

Your great enemy the empress has died, I understand in terrible pain, giving birth to a stillborn child. The emperor seems to be declining into the grave, young as he is, with grief for her. So they say: but perhaps he is simply declining under God's judgement, for we have had earthquakes and a terrifying hailstorm, and yet Arcadius will not relent and call you back even though he sees the destruction of his city, his family, his church and even his own life. I understand that the highest bishops in all the empire, even up to the Archbishop of Rome, have written urging him to turn back from his injustice, but to no effect.

I send you some money, some books and letters, some food and wine for your health, and pray all may reach you safely by the hand of my messenger, a faithful deacon who may cheer your soul for a few days and, I hope, bring back tidings from you in that far land. I hope he finds you well and in good spirits. As for me, I do my best to encourage the others in the church, but I myself grow faint and weary, often ill, and long to be out of this city. I dare not say I envy you, as I don't know what suffering you may be enduring now, but wherever you are, I'm glad you are out of the 'fiery furnace' of Constantinople.

All of your faithful followers — yours and Christ's — send their prayers and tears along with mine.

Olympias

To the most noble deaconess Olympias at Constantinople,
Fondest greetings to you from the desert reaches of Cappadocia.

I have been exiled to an even greater wilderness, west of here, but we are now breaking our journey during the harshness of winter.[1] The land where I find myself is rocky and almost barren of trees, grass, or fields. Strange stone pillars and porous caves form a landscape one might see in a dream. There is no escape from the cold, nor from the fierce pagan tribes that constantly attack the folk living in these parts. I have been met from time to time on this journey with kind and faithful Christians who have allowed me to stay in their comfortable homes, but each time we have been hurried on by the robbing tribes or by my enemies, who seem to be everywhere, threatening my life and those of the few faithful deacons and the guards who travel with us.

I cannot say I am much cheered by your letter, except knowing that you are remaining faithful, and that those who loved and supported me love and support me still, despite such hardship. But you must rest and allow yourself to recover, body and heart, if you are to be of great use to the church. As for me, my health is bad. There is a cold in my bones that cannot be warmed by any number of blankets or any size of fire — but my heart is strong and warm toward you all.

Who knows but that the reason for my time in Constantinople would have been to prepare you all for a time of suffering? Remember what Paul said, 'Think it not strange that some terrible thing should happen to you.' Why should we expect to live for Christ without sharing in his sufferings?

---

1. John was exiled across modern-day Turkey in an effort to make him impossible for his followers to reach. In that time he wrote and received hundreds of letters, and seventeen of his letters to Olympias still exist.

A few people have dared to find their way out to me here in my wilderness, and those that come bring books and papers. Some of these have been ancient epistles, newly circulated among bishops, which many believe to be part of God's inspired Word. I hear there are new letters found from Peter and John, which the church in the West have accepted as real and true. It may seem incredible that ancient letters from the apostles can still be read anew three hundred years after their writing, but of course God can preserve such messages, and who knows whether there may be some yet to be found? Of course, when we read any such document, we must discern whether it is faithful to the rest of the Holy Scriptures.

The most controversial of these books is the so-called Revelation of John, said to be the apostle John whom Jesus loved, written in exile on the Isle of Patmos. While dying, he writes that he saw great visions of what is to come. I have been reading this book here in my own exile. There is much in it that is mysterious, fantastical, even frightening; but there is also much that reminds one of the great prophecies of Daniel, which Jesus talked about in the Gospels. It is full of the glory of Christ as the Lamb who was killed as the great sacrifice, and there are pictures of the majesty and beauty of heaven that no mere man could have imagined. Is it a true Word of God, or simply a wonderful dream? I suppose it is not for an old man in a distant mountain place to make such a judgement, but I can tell you that it has filled my thoughts and my own dreams, and I am glad to have read it before I die.

In my opinion, one of the most convincing and important passages of Revelation is the opening section, in which our

Lord sends most solemn messages to seven of the first churches. And particularly striking to me is his message to the church of Smyrna:

The words of the first and the last, who died and came to life.

'Do not fear what you are about to suffer. Behold, the devil is about to throw some of you into prison, that you may be tested, and for ten days you will have tribulation. Be faithful until death, and I will give you the crown of life. He who has an ear, let him hear what the Spirit says to the churches. The one who conquers will not be hurt by the second death.'[2]

Were these words written by the beloved apostle? I say that they speak strongly of truth, and that they will encourage and strengthen all those who are weak and troubled in these dark days.[3] As for me, I can nearly see my crown now. I reach out my hand and grasp for it from my sickbed. You are right to envy me, dear lady, for it is not long before I will gain the victory and the greatest joy.

My deacons and the monks of these desert places have heard of your grace and faithfulness, and send your greetings.

John

---

2. Revelation 2:10-11.

3. We don't know whether John ever read Revelation – at this time most of the eastern empire's archbishops were just starting to receive copies and read it. Revelation is not actually referenced in any of John's sermons or writings, but it's interesting to remember that in A.D. 404 there were still parts of the Bible that were 'new'! Other books that were making their way across the empire were 2 Peter, 1 and 2 John, and Jude.

Three Years Later

It seemed amazing even to John that he was still alive. He had recovered from his 'frozen bones,' thawing as the ground thawed, and despite starvation and illnesses and attack by pagan tribes, had somehow continued living as if by the strength of God alone. He remembered old, blind Isaac in the book of Genesis, who had given his son Jacob his blessing in the firm belief he was dying, only to find himself still alive when Jacob found his way home twenty years later. John hoped he would not live so long.

'You are receiving too many letters and visitors and donations,' the harsher of his two guards told him one day. 'The emperor demands you be moved to a more deserted place. How can the city be united and peaceful when you are still wielding your dangerous influence there?'

'The emperor is dead, and his son, whom I baptised, is only a child,' John returned. 'Yet he demands my removal?'

'Yes!' the guard snapped. 'Get ready to move.'

John sighed and began to collect his books and papers together once more. Nothing changed in Constantinople: a weak emperor being controlled by the whims and furies of courtiers and politicians. No doubt the person really giving the order was another power-hungry Eutropius. Soon enough, no doubt, there would be another Eudokia to turn her husband's influence to her own interests. John reminded himself not to be cynical, and prayed for the young Theodosius II as he packed his things. Maybe he would be his own man, and not fall into the trap of his father. A sweet baby he'd been, though weighed down by the gold chains of the throne and the expectations of his mother.

John moved slowly these days, his joints and hands stiff, and he was only half packed when the guard came back. 'We move now,' he snapped. 'You leave whatever isn't packed. No point overloading the mule anyway.'

John took a last look at his other personal effects, his relatively comfortable room, but he shed no tears over it. He had never looked back long at any comfort. His whole life had been a journey with only one real destination, and he was getting close to that City which was his real home.

For weeks his mule plodded along the freezing, rocky road, John gritting his teeth as his skinny bones knocked against the mule's, bruising him; but he didn't have the strength to get off and walk.

One morning he felt much worse than usual. He could barely raise himself off the mat on which he'd spent a weary, hard night. 'Please,' he said. 'Another night or two to regain my strength. Have I ever resisted going with you? Just allow me one day to get well.'

One of the guards, who was inclined to be sympathetic to John's cause, looked worried. 'I don't suppose we're in a hurry to get to the Black Sea. We're not far now.'

'Another day waiting for the old man is another day we're stuck out here in the middle of nowhere,' the other guard growled through gritted teeth. 'Get up, heretic. The empire's business waits for no man.'

John tried, but he could only roll onto his knees. The two guards took him under the arms, one gently, the other roughly, and walked him outside and onto his mule.

John could barely even look up at the dramatic hills as his donkey walked on. The only time he raised his eyes was when he heard they were passing the shrine of the dead saint Basiliscus. Sure enough, there was a little grotto built up over a grave, marked by a cross, and a chapel nearby where a few monks stayed to pay honour to this man of God and to imitate his life of faith. As they slowly passed the shrine, John heard a voice in his head: *Be of good cheer, brother. Tomorrow we will be together.* Unseen by his guards, John faintly smiled.

A quarter mile on, still smiling, John dropped from his mule. The two guards stopped and stared at each other.

'We'd better go back,' the gentler one said.

'All the way to Comana?'

'What else can we do?'

'Let's go to the shrine we just passed. Those monks will set him right.'

They turned to make the journey back to where they could still see the chapel in the distance and called loudly for the monks to come out and help.

The monks, emerging to see who had come to disturb them, were startled to see two soldiers on their horses outside their cave.

'Has there been some trouble?' a monk asked, staring nervously from one guard to the other.

'No,' the gentler soldier said decidedly. 'We need your help. We are escorting this man on his exile and he's fallen ill on the way.'

'It is our business to care for the ill,' the monk replied. 'Bring him in. A criminal?'

'Yes,' the rough guard said.

'A preacher,' the other replied. 'He was the archbishop until he made an enemy of the empress – the former empress, I should say.'

'This is John of Antioch!' the monk gasped. 'Bring him in at once. But you must wait outside. Men of war are not allowed inside our cells.'

'Precious little entertainment in there, I should think,' the rough guard said, yawning. 'Let us know when he's settled so we can ride back to town and get a drink.'

The monk didn't answer. He was too busy carrying John inside with the others.

Despite the soldiers' request, it was hours before the monk came out again.

'The archbishop is dead,' he said. 'His last words were "Glory to God for all things."' The man's face was wet with tears, but happy tears, his smile lighting up his face. 'We must bury him in our shrine along with the saint.'

'Do what you want with his body, but let us see it first,' the rough guard replied. 'We have to testify he's dead. Then we're free of him – couldn't have planned it better. No seaside for us, lad, eh! Back to the capital at last – civilisation!' It was the first time he'd smiled for days.

The monks carried out the body, already wrapped in a clean white robe. It was indeed the old man that the soldiers had spent three years guarding, his face still and peaceful.

'He was a very great man,' the gentle guard said. 'I don't doubt he spent many prayers on us.'

'For all that matters, coming from an old heretic.'

The gentle guard shook his head. 'Any man who could die with those words on his lips is no heretic.' He handed the monk a few coins. 'For the burial. Thank you for your kindness.'

'You've gone soft,' his friend muttered. 'Since when do you care about the old preacher?'

'Since I saw a man who showed me Christ even in suffering. Didn't you see anything of what I saw in him?'

The two men waved to the monks and mounted their horses, riding due west, where the sun was setting over Constantinople. It would be a long conversation for a long journey.

Thinking Further Topics

A Night Out on the Town

Basil reminds John that Jesus gave his life for us, and asks him to consider giving up his comfortable life to give his all back to Jesus. Do you know Jesus as the One who came to save you? What are some of the dreams you have for your life – do they feel like the most important thing, or do you think you could give them up if God called you to serve him in another way?

A New Life

One of the ways to serve God is just by being a good son or daughter. That's one place you can start serving him now! What are some of the ways you're a good child to your parents, and where can you improve? How can knowing Jesus help you to do better?

Losing a Friend, Gaining a Minister

Did John do the right thing or the wrong thing in leading Basil believe he was also going to become a preacher? Do you think his actions grew their friendship deeper, or hurt it?

Leaving Home

Take five minutes to think just about Jesus and prayer. Do you think you could do just that by yourself for two years?! Is there a point to these monks who go out into the wilderness to be alone with God – does anyone in the Bible do it? Some of the monks had an extreme lifestyle like keeping themselves from sleep, warmth and food. Is that a good idea or a bad one?

The First Christmas in Antioch

Even at the very first Christmas celebrated in Antioch, John noticed that the people were getting so caught up in all the parties and preparations that they forgot 'the reason for the season'! What are some of your favourite things about Christmas? What are some ways we can use it to focus more on Jesus and the reason why he came – to save us?

Riots in the Street

Why are people often more interested in God or Church when they're going through a really tough or scary time? How can we use John's example to help point them to Jesus during those times, and to be braver ourselves?

Kidnapped

I wonder if your minister was kidnapped by the government and forced to lead your church! Of course that doesn't really happen to people today – but being called by God can feel a little similar. Sometimes God calls people where they would never expect, or don't really want to go. How might you know it if God were calling you to a new place or new way to serve? Can you find some verses about how God leads us?

A New Home

John is horrified to see how fancy his new home is and how much money is wasted on it. How would you feel if you were given a new home and found out it was a palace? What are some ways you could use it to serve people instead of having it all to yourself?

Meeting Constantinople

John, Serapion and Olympias give their dinner to the poor outside the archbishop's palace. Serving sick, poor or homeless people can be really tough – and really rewarding too. What are some reasons why we should do it? What does the Bible say about how we should treat the poor?

The Archbishop's Staff

John gives his priests and bishops a good telling off for three things – what are they? Is he right to give them such a hard time, or is he a bit extreme? Do you think you'd like working for him?

John and the Heretics

How do we know from the Bible that the Arians are wrong to believe Jesus was born as just a human and later became God? In this chapter John instructs his followers to be kind to the Arians and to peacefully protest against them – how do you deal with people you think are wrong, or who don't know the truth about Jesus?

Enemies in the Palace
Why is Eudokia so upset that John disapproves of her friends? What things are most important to Eutropius? They are both mostly interested in John because of what he can do for them – how do you deal with people like that?

Sanctuary
Eutropius has fallen from the very height of power to a place where he could lose his life. Can you think of any times in real life or in the Bible where that has happened to somebody? There are lots of people who were once famous but who aren't popular anymore. How should that change the way we think about success in this world?

A Special Audience for a Special Sermon
How do you think Eutropius felt when John preached about him – right in front of him?! What would you have said to someone in his position, especially if that someone had been your enemy?

The Tall Brothers
Theophilus was known to be greedy, untruthful, and hold grudges against people who had offended him.

What are some verses in the Bible that tell us what characteristics a Christian should show instead? What kind of character would you want to be known for?

Theophilus Turns the Tables

Theophilus doesn't act like we expect a church leader to! What are some of the things he's done that are wrong? If he believed John were really a bad man, how does the Bible say we should deal with people who are acting sinfully?

Judgement

Do you think the charges against John are true or not? How did it make you feel whenever someone has said something untrue about you? Why is he so happy to be going through the same kind of trial as Jesus? See Acts 5:41.

The Last Sermon

John has reacted to injustice by continuing to serve where God has placed him. How do you react when something unfair has happened to you or hasn't gone your way? How do you weigh up your 'rights' against acting in a Christlike way?

The City Without John

Do you think God really sent an earthquake or tragedy to punish the emperor for unjustly exiling John? Why do you think the emperor really sent him away?

Back to the City – Questions

John doesn't go back into his job right away because he's afraid of the same thing happening all over again. Is he being wise or fearful? How can we find the right balance in being 'wise as serpents but gentle as doves'? John arriving back in the city gives a picture of arriving into heaven. What do you think it might be like?

A New Storm – Questions

John compares Eudokia to Herodias, the wife of the King Herod who had John the Baptist killed. In what ways are the two women alike? In what ways was John like John the Baptist? In some ways he might have been right, but perhaps he wasn't very wise to say this. When we see our leaders acting in wicked ways, what are some ways we can react?

War Against the Church – Questions

Imagine living in a country where Christians and churches are persecuted, even killed. Do you think you would have the courage to keep coming back? Many churches today really are persecuted like this. Look up the underground church in China, or Christians in middle eastern countries, and take some time to pray for them.

Letters in Exile – Questions

Today Christians believe that we have the complete Bible and that God's Word cannot have any more additions. Sometimes people claim that they've found a new book of the Bible. How do we test whether they're right or wrong? What do you think it would have been like to read Revelation for the first time – does it sound like the rest of the Bible or really different?

Three Years Later – Questions
Are you afraid of dying? How can God give you strength when you're afraid? Do you live in such a way that even your enemies, like John's guards, would see Jesus through your life?

Life Summary

John was born in Antioch about A.D. 343. His father died before he was born and he was raised by his Christian mother, Anthusa, who sacrificed to send him for an excellent education. As a young man he was set to become the most famous orator (speaker, or lawyer) in the city, but his friend Basil pointed him to Christ and persuaded him to devote himself to the things of God. After his mother's death, John became a monk in the desert, including two years in complete isolation, but had to return to the city when his health suffered.

Back in Antioch John became a reader, then deacon, then priest, and was well-known for his powerful sermons. During this time he preached at Antioch's first ever Christmas services, and became famous for a series of sermons he preached after Antioch rioted against the emperor. As a result of his powers of persuasion, he was kidnapped and forced to become Archbishop of Constantinople.

While he was well-liked in Constantinople to start with, he soon found enemies in the weak emperor Arcadius, his superstitious wife Eudokia, and the ruthless chamberlain Eutrophius. Their dislike of him contributed to his downfall when the vengeful Archbishop of Alexandria, Theophilus, accused John of many made-up charges in the Council of the Oak. John was sentenced to exile, but called back by the emperor after riots and earthquakes frightened the empress. His triumph was short-lived, however, and he was exiled again several months later after offending Eudokia all over again. John lived three years in exile and died in the mountainous desert of Cappadocia. After his death Arcadius' son, Theodosius II, had his body brought back to Constantinople and honoured. John's legacy survived through his many recorded sermons, and generations later he became known as 'Chrysostom', or the 'Golden Mouth'.

John Chrysostom Timeline

A.D.

343   John Chrysostom born.

367   Theodosius I becomes emperor
after the last pagan Byzantine
emperor, Julian the Apostate, dies.

368   John leaves his studies with the pagan
philosopher Libanius and is baptised.

372-378 John becomes a monk in the desert.

378   John returns to Antioch and becomes
a reader (like a deacon) under the
bishop Flavian; ordained priest in
385 or 386.

386   Christmas is first celebrated in Antioch.

387   Riots break out in Antioch over new
taxation.

395   Theodosius dies; Arcadius becomes
emperor in the east (Byzantium),
Honorius in the west (Rome).

398   John is installed as Archbishop of
Constantinople.

399   Eutropius takes sanctuary in Hagia
Sophia, captured by soldiers a week later.

402	Theophilus arrives in Constantinople.
403	John's first exile, lasting about three days.
404	Eudokia raises monument to herself in the Augusteion.
Easter 404	Imperial forces attack three different services led by John and his priests. John goes into second exile; Hagia Sophia burned to the ground along with much of the city.
Sept 407	John dies and is buried in the shrine of Bishop Basiliscus, in Comana.
438	John's body is exhumed and brought to Constantinople, where the mourning for him is led by Arcadius and Eudokia's son Theodosius II, whom John had baptised as an infant.

Terms and Characters

Aelia Eudoxia (pronounced Eudokia) – Arcadius' superstitious queen.

Anthusa – John's mother, a Christian lady who had been a widow since about the age of eighteen.

Arcadius – Theodosius' eldest son, and the emperor when John went to Constantinople.

Basil – John's best friend, who persuades him to give up his legal career to devote himself to God (may be fictional).

Basileus/Basilissa – the correct form of address to a Byzantine emperor.

Briso – a chamberlain and friend of John's.

Eutropius – the most important chamberlain (civil servant) in Arcadius' court. He had set up Arcadius' marriage to Eudokia and was ruthlessly hungry for more and more power.

Flavian – the bishop under whom John first worked as a priest in Antioch.

Isidore – a bishop whom Theophilus had backed to become archbishop of Constantinople before they fell out; a friend of the Tall Brothers.

Libanius – John's pagan tutor, the cleverest man in Antioch. Had also tutored the emperor, Julian the Apostate.

Olympias – a beautiful and wealthy deaconess, or female servant of the Church, she had a close friendship with John and wrote him many letters in exile.

Origen – an early church writer with some crazy ideas. His writings were used as the excuse to persecute many in the Church, including John.

Serapion – John's archdeacon; basically the chief administrator in the parish of Constantinople.

Severian – not to be confused with Serapion, he was a bishop from out of town who fell out with John.

Theodosius I – the emperor when John first entered the ministry, he was known for his hot temper. Today he is best remembered for the striking city walls he had built around Constantinople.

Theophilus – the archbishop of Alexandria, Egypt, and John's greatest enemy.

The Tall Brothers – three Egyptian monks who had been persecuted by Theophilus. Their complaint led to the trial that finally exiled John.

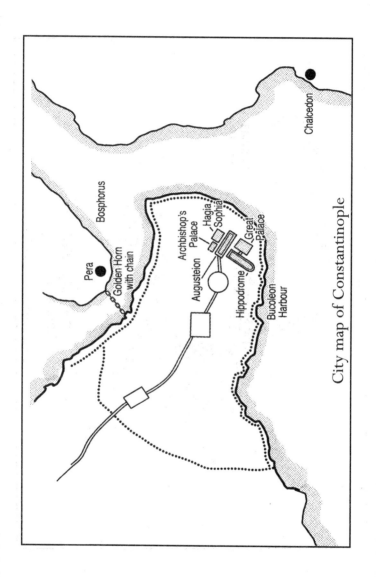

City map of Constantinople

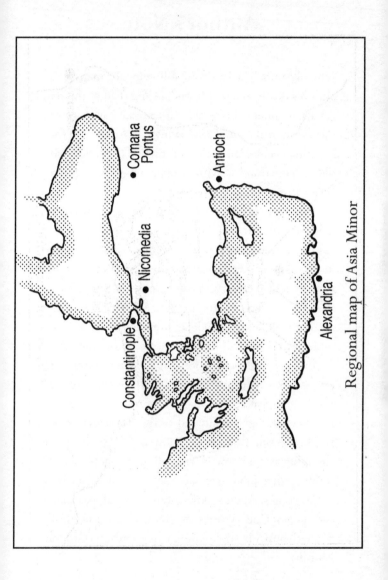

Regional map of Asia Minor

177

Author's Note

John of Antioch had a strong following for many years after his death, and is still studied and read to this day. A huge number of his essays and sermons have survived (far more than I could read in my research!), and they are still excellent and relevant, though the style is a bit old-fashioned and, as with most preachers, one doesn't agree with every point of doctrine.

John was a product of his time – a time in which the church, still influenced by pagan traditions, practiced respect toward icons, prayed to dead saints, believed in punishment for Christians after death, and (in the case of monks) underwent severe physical punishments in order to overcome temptation. Most of these things are impossible for a modern, evangelical Christian to understand; after all, they are not found in the Bible.

But we must remember that the Church, just like society, has naturally changed and grown over the years, and that it was the corruption of these very practices that eventually led to the Reformation and the Protestant Church we know today. At this point the Bible as we know it was still incomplete, and it's unlikely that John ever saw the book of Revelation, among others. Yet it was his intense, literal, passionate teaching of God's Word that, centuries after his death, earned him his nickname: Chrysostom (Golden-Mouth).

For some ten years now I have wanted to write a book set in ancient Constantinople. The Byzantine Empire, while not very popular today, is my favourite period of history. Lasting from A.D. 330 to 1453, it's one of the longest-lasting empires of world history, and yet is known by most people for little more than inventing the fork. In reality it was a continuation of the Roman Empire, but was even more glamorous, sophisticated and dramatic.

The reason behind my fascination with Constantinople is the way its history still lives in the streets of modern-day Istanbul. The outline of the Hippodrome has been preserved, along with the monuments of the central barrier; and of course the famous cathedral of Hagia Sophia, rebuilt in its current form by the emperor Justinian some two hundred and fifty years after John Chrysostom's death, stands on the site of the original church. The mosaic floors of aristocratic homes and the great chain that stretched across the Golden Horn are housed in Istanbul's museums, along with many other artefacts from the ancient city. Much of the land and sea walls are still intact, along with a small part of the royal harbour of Bucoleon, and even some of the street layout is unchanged, marked by ancient monuments. You can walk the streets of Istanbul and feel that you are walking with John and Serapion.

For anyone wishing to discover more about Byzantium, I would highly recommend John Julius

Norwich's *History of Byzantium*. I have read and consulted more books about the empire than I can list here (and even used a Byzantine cookbook to try out some ancient recipes!), but Norwich's books were the first and still the best. I also love *Byzantium 1200*, a book and website produced by an archaeological project of the same name, that acts as a guidebook to the ancient city in the midst of the modern. Unfortunately, there is no modern, complete book available on the life and works of Chrysostom, but some books that I have found helpful were *St John Chrysostom,* by Donald Attwater, and *John Chrysostom (Bitesize Biographies)* by Earl Blackburn.

I would like to thank Dr Matthew Hoskin, an expert on early church history, for his help in editing this book, as well as my faithful critique partners, Karen Murdarasi and Esther Nixon, and my supportive editor Catherine Mackenzie. Above all I thank my husband, Neil, who was obsessed with Byzantium long before I was, and passed it on to me when he took me to Istanbul on our honeymoon. We have had many long, happy conversations along the line of 'Who's your favourite emperor?' and have travelled far and wide to go to Byzantine exhibitions and lectures. Every couple needs a hobby!

In writing about John Chrysostom, what I found challenging for my own life were his complete dedication of his life to Christ's service, without compromise or regret; his thorough knowledge of the Bible and gifts in helping others to apply it; his understanding of how little the world and its pleasures can really offer us; and his fearlessness despite personal injustice and suffering. These are examples that each of us must follow in the face of the world's opposition. I pray that you will do so, dear reader, and ask you to pray that I will too!

About the Author

Dayspring MacLeod lives in Scotland with her husband and three children. She is an editor, author and ghostwriter, and in her spare time – she writes novels! When not in front of her laptop or watching Disney movies with her kids, she can be found in the kitchen, making American treats she remembers from her childhood in Michigan. Dayspring loves Jesus and wants to help both young and older readers see his beauty and truth through her writing.

Do the Next Thing: Elisabeth Elliot

by Selah Helms

- The story of an inspirational woman
- Courage in the face of grief
- Part of the Trailblazers biography series
-

Although she is best known for her time on the mission field in Ecuador, Elisabeth Elliot went on to become a vibrant role model for valiant, godly women all over the world. Follow her journey from the jungles of the Amazon, where she faced the tragic death of her first husband, to the lecture halls and radio shows of the culture wars, where she stood as a strong defender of God's Word.

ISBN: 978-1-5271-0161-6

OTHER BOOKS IN THE
TRAIL BLAZERS SERIES

For a full list of Trail Blazers, please see our
website: www.christianfocus.com
All Trail Blazers are available as e-books

• Wilfred Grenfell •

COURAGEOUS DOCTOR

Linda Finlayson

Courageous Doctor: Wilfred Grenfell

by Linda Finlayson

'Faster, Jack, faster!' Wilfred Grenfell called to the lead dog in his sledge team. Jack needed no second reminder. He loved to go as fast as possible and he urged his team forward. Wilfred loved to go fast too, and felt a thrill as the cold wind blew past his face. There was such freedom flying across deep snow and ice, and so far, all seemed to be going well. But just then, instead of hard ice, they hit slush, which meant a patch of ice was melting and could break apart at any moment. 'Come on Jack,' Wilfred yelled. 'Faster!' But it did not matter. The worst thing happened. Right in front of the dogs the ice cracked open. Watching in horror, Jack and then one by one the other dogs, slid into the freezing water ...

ISBN: 978-1-5271-0173-9

A Love for the Lost: David Brainerd

by Brian H. Cosby

Life on the American frontier in the early 1700s was very difficult – continually threatened by disease, attack, and brutally cold winters. The English and Native Americans lived side by side, which often led to conflict. David Brainerd arose as a compassionate and fearless missionary to the various Indian tribes in America. Riding on his horse across rivers, over mountains, and through towns, Brainerd carried the gospel of Jesus Christ to the lost, the hurting, and the broken. Notable pastors and missionaries like John Wesley, William Carey, Adoniram Judson and Jim Elliot were all influenced by the life, passion, and dedication of David Brainerd. In this book, Brian Cosby takes the reader on a journey from Brainerd's teenage years on the farm to his expulsion from Yale; from preaching on the frontier to his death in his late 20s. The reader will be encouraged, inspired, and challenged by the perseverance and single-minded devotion of the early American missionary to the Indians, David Brainerd.

ISBN: 978-1-84550-695-7

TRAIL BLAZERS

• Isobel Kuhn •

LIGHTS IN
LISULAND

Irene Howat

Lights in Lisuland: Isobel Kuhn

by Irene Howat

Isobel Kuhn wasn't always a missionary – she wasn't always a Christian.

Her teachers discouraged a belief in God and promoted evolution. Isobel sometimes doubted whether there was anybody there at all to hear her prayers. 'They don't go beyond the ceiling you know,' she once said to her father who was desperately praying for his young daughter.

Isobel even considered suicide once but the thought of her parents' heartache stopped her.

Discover what brought this questioning, antagonistic teenager from doubts to faith in Christ. Find out how she affected the lives of countless people on the mission field of China and Thailand.

This stirring and challenging story of faith is a role model to young people everywhere.

ISBN: 978-1-85792-610-1

CHRISTIAN FOCUS PUBLICATIONS

Christian Focus | Christian Heritage | CF4K | Mentor

Christian Focus Publications publishes books for adults and children under its four main imprints: Christian Focus, CF4K, Mentor and Christian Heritage. Our books reflect our conviction that God's Word is reliable and Jesus is the way to know him, and live for ever with him.

Our children's publication list includes a Sunday School curriculum that covers pre-school to early teens, and puzzle and activity books. We also publish personal and family devotional titles, biographies and inspirational stories that children will love.

If you are looking for quality Bible teaching for children then we have an excellent range of Bible stories and age-specific theological books.

From pre-school board books to teenage apologetics, we have it covered!

Find us at our web page:
www.christianfocus.com

CF4·K
Because you're never
too young to know Jesus